Praise for *The Genius Habit*

"Give yourself the gift of genius—not through inborn luck, but through Laura Garnett's powerful, practical system to build a lifelong Genius Habit. Bored at work? Instead of berating yourself, consider that your plateaus are signals pointing toward greater purpose. This book will help you dismantle barriers to find what really lights you up as you click into the contagious joy of doing the work you—and only you—were born to do."

—Jenny Blake, author of *Pivot: The Only Move That Matters Is Your Next One*

"Work doesn't have to feel like, well, work. With Laura's advice, you can find your Zone of Genius, accomplish more, and stop counting the minutes until quitting time."

—Laura Vanderkam, author of *Off the Clock: Feel Less Busy While Getting More Done*

"Laura Garnett has written a powerful guide to finding and sustaining success and joy in your work. She has helped me and many other people get in touch with our essence and our unique gifts and coached us on how to live and work in that zone for an ever-growing proportion of our lives. The results are nothing short of astounding on all fronts. Life can hold so much more satisfaction and delight than we can imagine, and this book shows us how to unlock that."

—Raj Sisodia, cofounder and chairman emeritus of Conscious Capitalism International

"Among the most hopeful—and useful—ideas detailed in this book is that genius is a habit one can cultivate and a process one can commit to. Whether you are a young professional just starting your climb up the corporate ladder, an evolved businessperson, or a midcareer expert who wants to be an entrepreneur, Laura Garnett's book is the voice of a patient, highly intelligent mentor who can significantly expand your own capabilities."

—Vineet Nayar, founder and chairman of the Sampark Foundation and bestselling author of *Employees First, Customers Second*

"Loving your job and career shouldn't feel like a struggle. Instead, it should be about finding and harnessing your true greatness. In *The Genius Habit*, Laura Garnett shows you exactly how to do this while inspiring and helping others along the way."

—Dorie Clark, author of *Entrepreneurial You* and *Stand Out*

"Laura Garnett's genius is that she not only understands that careers are nonlinear, but she provides the GPS to discovering your purpose and your genius, which will unlock your gifts and make work an inspiring journey."

—David S. Kidder, cofounder and CEO of Bionic and *New York Times* bestselling author of *The Intellectual Devotional* and *The Startup Playbook*

"There is a genius hiding in all of us, and if you haven't found yours, you are probably dreading every Monday morning drive to work. Most of us go a lifetime searching for joy at work. Finding your genius is the key. It turns out there is a genius habit you can develop, and Laura Garnett shows us how. In following her timeless advice, we can get to the joy we always dreamed was possible and become the person we were destined to be."

—Rich Sheridan, author of *Joy, Inc.* and *Chief Joy Officer*

THE
GENIUS
HABIT

THE GENIUS HABIT

HOW *ONE HABIT* CAN RADICALLY
CHANGE YOUR WORK AND YOUR LIFE

LAURA GARNETT

Published by Sourcebooks, Inc.
P.O. Box 4410, Naperville, Illinois 60563-4410
(630) 961-3900
Fax: (630) 961-2168
sourcebooks.com

Library of Congress Cataloging-in-Publication Data

Names: Garnett, Laura, author.
Title: The genius habit : how one habit can radically change your work and
    your life / Laura Garnett.
Description: Naperville : Sourcebooks, Inc., [2019] | Includes
    bibliographical references.
Identifiers: LCCN 2018033684 | (hardcover : alk. paper)
Subjects: LCSH: Career development. | Job satisfaction.
Classification: LCC HF5381 .G277 2019 | DDC 650.1--dc23
LC record available at https://lccn.loc.gov/2018033684

Printed and bound in the United States of America.
WOZ 10 9 8 7 6 5 4 3 2 1

For Zoe and James—for seeing me always.

"The privilege of a lifetime is being who you are."

—Joseph Campbell

TABLE OF CONTENTS

INTRODUCTION

Not long ago, I attended a dinner party while on a business trip in San Francisco. The hosts' home was beautiful, one that only the elite would dream of owning. It was perfect, tastefully decorated with modern, comfortable furniture. The view of the Golden Gate Bridge was stunning, and the dining room was exquisitely set for ten.

My hosts, who worked hard for their money and status, were some of the most down-to-earth and fun people I'd met. Their friends were in the same boat—affluent and paying for private schools for their children, which is no small feat. Everyone in attendance dressed impeccably and had impressive resumes. I had expected the usual dinner party banter about who works where and how we were connected. But when we sat down to dinner, one of the hosts wanted to play a game. She said, "Here's a question I thought we could all answer. If you could change careers and have any job you wanted, what would it be?"

You would think, based on their level of success and wealth, that these people would be satisfied and happy with their jobs; after all, they excelled in careers that the majority of us would covet. Yet almost everyone at the table shared a desire to do something different with their lives. They clearly weren't in love with their work. One lawyer wanted to be a musician, while the tech industry executives wanted to be writers. Each spouse seemed visibly nervous as they listened to their partners' revelations. It was obvious they'd never admitted these things to one another before. Perhaps the thought of losing even a drop of income scared them. Their lifestyles dictated the need for high-paying jobs, regardless of whether they really enjoyed what they were doing.

When it was my turn, I said, "Actually, I wouldn't change a thing. I'm doing exactly what I want."

"Oh, please," said the marketing executive sitting next to me. "Come on, nobody is *that* happy with work." There were murmurs of agreement from others at the table.

So many people have regret or unfulfilled dreams regarding their careers that many are shocked when I say how much I love my job—it's just not something you hear very often. In fact, I don't just love my job; my work is an extension of who I am and pushes me to be who I want to be. It is my constant source of energy. In fact, when I was experiencing overwhelming sickness during my first trimester of pregnancy, my work gave me strength to carry on. Seriously, I look forward to work more than vacation, and when I am on vacation, although delighted, I'm eager to get back to work. I feel like every day is Friday, and I don't want the weekends to start. I don't daydream about what I could be doing with my career or life because I'm already doing it. I never thought it would be possible to feel this way about my job—but I do.

While what I just described may sound idyllic, it did not come easily. Creating a job to which I'm truly and emotionally attached required a lot of work. I've always been ambitious; however, I had no clue what I wanted to do with my life after college. Throughout my childhood, I was taught that the path to success was paved with good grades, college, and a job—any well-paying job. My parents rarely talked about prioritizing happiness or job satisfaction. What really mattered was financial security.

Even though I knew the rules I was supposed to follow, my path was a bit different. I spent two years after college exploring: I waited tables, then moved to Holland to be an au pair, then came back home and started a master's degree in nutrition. While nutrition was a passion of mine, I discovered that working with people to help them build basic healthy behaviors was boring, and it didn't provide the right challenge for me. I soon abandoned that opportunity, moved to Richmond, Virginia, and got a job at a wine distribution company as an administrative assistant. I had my eye on another position within the industry: wine sales. I figured if I worked really hard and did my absolute best, the powers that be would recognize my initiative and promote me. Even though I was bored with the work, I spent day after day filing invoices, and what I didn't finish during the day I would take home at night, trying to prove my worth to the CEO. I didn't know who I was and I didn't know what I was good at, but I knew I was expected to do whatever it took to get the job done.

One day, the CEO called me into his office. He said, "You know what, Laura? We think that you're too qualified for this job and we don't have the budget for your position anymore, so we're letting you go. I think you're going to be better off doing something else."

As much as it hurt, I knew he was right. That job was not right for me; it wasn't really my calling. As I will say many times in this book, it's often a blessing when you get fired or get kicked out of a job. The push to move on is something to embrace because it means the job was not right for you. In the moment, however, I saw it as total rejection.

I ran out of the office in tears and decided I had to find a new job immediately. Serendipitously, I ran into a friend who was working at Capital One and told me the international bank was expanding rapidly. At the time, they had a unique corporate philosophy on hiring: they didn't emphasize experience or credentials. Instead, they relied on an extremely rigorous interview process. If you passed a series of tests—logic, math, and more— you were a potential candidate.

I was hired as a marketing manager. They offered me a salary I previously couldn't even have imagined, exponentially higher than anything I had earned before. I remember jumping up and down, screaming with joy and feeling like my life had just started.

Capital One's philosophy was that you could learn on the job, which was great because I'd never done marketing before. My undergraduate degree was a major in political science with a minor in sociology; I knew I was good at critical thinking, but I had no marketing strategy background. Once I got there, I ramped up my efforts to succeed at the job, and I learned as I went. Over time, lots of opportunities came my way. Eventually I applied to join the Marketing and Analysis group, which at Capital One was the crème de la crème. That's where all the best people were. I decided I needed to be in this top-notch department because it would look good on my résumé. It would also make me feel important and smart.

I was hired into the department and moved to Washington, DC. Within three weeks of my arrival, the management team decided to dissolve my group. But this was in the heyday of Capital One, so the restructuring was actually an amazing opportunity. If anything, it was a huge door opener because my manager asked me, "What do you want to do next?"

I had the travel bug, so I answered, "What are we doing

internationally? How can I get on an international team?" There was one small group in South Africa that was hiring, and two weeks later, I got on a plane. I lived in South Africa for two years. The group was highly entrepreneurial in the sense that we were building a business from scratch. Every day I was tackling the jobs of twenty-five people back in the United States. It was a huge confidence builder for me because I was thriving, I was excited, and I was adding value. On top of that I met a guy, fell in love, and got married. He was also working for Capital One and living in South Africa for a short stint.

From there we were both sent to Spain, London, and finally Washington, DC, and that's where the Capital One party ended. Once we were back in the United States, I felt more like I was working for a large organization, which was completely different from the international start-ups. It didn't take long in my new role to realize I wasn't having fun anymore. I was uninspired by the tasks and projects I was managing. I didn't see how what I did made any real difference or impact on the business. I had a job that was largely operational, not strategic, and I lost all energy and enthusiasm for going to work. I was bored, uninspired, and even more upsetting, I didn't see a role that I wanted to move into. My husband felt similarly, and we decided to move on. We packed our bags and moved to New York.

Within a month, I ended up at Google in a sales job, and I was ecstatic—at first. In 2005, Google was *the* company to work for, and it immediately gave me bragging rights. Yet to my dismay, the moment I got there I knew it was a terrible fit. I lacked autonomy—I had to respond immediately to clients' needs, which seemed never-ending, and I had little control over my day-to-day work. I had also been demoted. While I had led a team of five people at Capital One, at Google I was an individual contributor on a sales team with no management opportunities. When it became clear that the job wasn't a good fit, I blamed myself: perhaps I wasn't as thorough in the interview process as I should have been, I had been starry-eyed about the possibility of working at Google, I didn't enjoy the job search and wanted to get back to work as quickly as possible. In the end, I had made a mistake many people make over and over by taking the first job that came my way. And because that job happened to be at Google, one of the most prestigious companies in the world, I didn't stop long enough to ask myself if it was the right job for *me*.

For the first time in my life I experienced something that I had only heard about from others: I dreaded going to work. It was a hard time for me—I hated my job, and on top of that, my marriage was beginning to crumble.

Rather than look for another job, I decided to stick it out and stay in my role for a year, knowing that I could then switch departments. After the first year, I applied to another position that seemed like a better fit—and for the first ten months it was. I also got divorced and was doing the work to move on with my life. I was excited about work again, but my happiness was short-lived. My department went through a reorganization, and my job changed. I was now back in a role that wasn't right for me. My manager was not supportive, and I struggled to find another opportunity within the company. I also noticed that I was getting sick on a regular basis. Once a month, I came down with a high fever and couldn't get out of bed for days. Worried that something was wrong with my health, I met with a litany of doctors and took a number of blood tests, all of which came back negative. According to my doctors, I was fine. So I pushed forward. I kept thinking, *If I try harder, maybe I can succeed here. Maybe I can make my weaknesses stronger. Maybe I can fit in.*

Even though I knew I was in the wrong job, I was addicted to the benefits: free food, free drinks, free snacks, and five-dollar massages (I think I got one every other day). My manager started talking to me about my "inability to succeed" in my role. I knew this job was not something I was good at, but I just couldn't stomach the idea of failure. I was put on a performance plan, which was crushing. I started thinking, *I'm thirty-three. What is the work that I'm really meant to do? Why haven't I figured this out yet?*

When we are dissatisfied with work, we're taught to seek answers outside of ourselves, to rely on feedback, advice, and the opinions of others. When I was looking for answers, I worked with coaches and read career books, trying to figure out who I was. The ideas I picked up sometimes resonated, and sometimes didn't.

Back at the Google office, I went to hear bestselling author Srikumar Rao speak. He asked the crowd, "Can you imagine waking up every morning and getting on your hands and knees and being so grateful for the job and life that you have that you're almost in tears of joy every morning?" I wanted *that* feeling, and I knew I didn't have it, even though to the outside world it looked like everything in my life was going fine. Any observer would have said, "Laura is a high achiever. She's worked for some of the best companies in the world. She's making it happen."

But I wasn't. I questioned everything. *What am I best at? What am I meant to do? How can I create the kind of career and success I dream about?* I read every book I could find on career and success and struggled to find concrete answers. I started an exhaustive job search, found a job quickly at a start-up, and quit Google. The start-up was short lived. I was there for nine months, but within a month, I knew that I was in another job that wasn't a great fit. I felt frustrated and as though I would never be able to find work that was right for me. I questioned my future, my value, and myself. Then, I got laid off. I will never forget that day—I was escorted out of the Frank Gehry building and in that moment, I decided that if my dream job doesn't exist, I was going to create it from scratch.

Miraculously, a few weeks before I got laid off, I got a call from Srikumar Rao, whom I had seen speak several times since his talk at Google. I had approached him after one of those talks and said that I was interested in working for him. Now he was calling to take me up on that offer, and I was ecstatic! I thought my dream job had landed in my lap. In my role as his head of sales and operations, I helped him grow his business of helping people get happy. Throughout my time working with him, I watched and learned. He taught me the valuable lesson that achieving happiness is not just something bestowed upon lucky people. Instead, happiness comes with daily practice; it is a habit you can cultivate. When I realized that my happiness was up to me, I worked every day on owning my power and my confidence, and soon after, happiness began to come. Developing this habit of creating my own happiness was an essential building block to me being able to create the work that I do now.

After working with Srikumar Rao, as well as another bestselling author in the personal growth field, I was ready for a complete pivot. I realized that working with them wasn't really my calling. I knew I wanted to work with entrepreneurs, but on my own terms. I found that the part of my business I enjoyed most was brand-building. I realized that in order to build a successful brand, you have to know who you are. And when I dug deeper, over time I realized it wasn't the actual branding that excited me; it was discovering who my clients were and how they could use this information to enhance their overall career, not just growing their small businesses. Once I realized it was careers that I wanted to focus on, I pivoted again. I went back to my corporate roots and targeted leaders who were in the corporate world.

I started working with individuals in large, medium, and small organizations, and helped them with their performance at work so that they could know who they were, own their performance, and build an exciting career, rather than aimlessly going from job to job. Meanwhile, I was also practicing what I was preaching by doing the work of building my confidence, getting more mindful, persevering through failures and tracking the moments when I was in the zone, and shifting my work and business to gain alignment. I noticed that when I did this, my joy increased and work became more fun. I began to see that I had the ability to shape my work experience more than I had ever realized. As I started to reject the assumptions I had about work and advice from others that didn't feel right, my whole life changed. Through this process, the unique insights and tracking methodology I use with my clients today slowly emerged, and my business started to really take off. My methodology for maximizing career potential was born.

My business grew through lots of trial and error, and along the way I realized that the moments when I enjoyed my work the most, when I was in the zone, occurred when I was asking people questions and seeing patterns in their responses that turned into insights and ultimately actionable steps they could use to create positive change. This was the work and the thinking that really lit me up. Whenever I did it, I completely lost track of time and felt as though I was on fire. Over time I found I could easily create more of these moments each day where I could use my unique way of problem-solving. I turned this way of proactively creating work that was aligned with who I was into a habit. The more I practiced it, the stronger it became, and the more challenged and fulfilled I felt about my work.

In the early days of starting my business, my parents were worried that I was never going to make enough money working for myself and that I was going to be homeless; my brother was telling me I needed to get an MBA before I put out my shingle. But I knew that it was time for me to challenge the norms of what I believed about work and career and start trusting myself.

All I had in terms of support was a tiny network of two other brave women who had also decided to start their own businesses. The three of us would meet at cafes, sharing what we were doing and supporting one another. I had some savings and used a portion of that money to keep me afloat. After a few years of hard work, I had a roster of clients, both individual and corporate. Coincidentally, Capital One was one of my first.

Today, I consider myself to be a successful performance strategist. I have become an expert in helping people understand the specific behaviors and habits required to perform at a very high level in their chosen careers. I've synthesized all the latest research and distilled the groundbreaking thinking from across industries into a process that allows people to incorporate these lessons into their lives. By using these tools, my clients learn that the key to achieving their best life and a job they love is to really understand who they are and what they are best at, and to take this knowledge and implement it inside of their work every day. By doing so, anyone can take more ownership of their career.

Is Happiness at Work Even Possible?

You may have experienced all the things I've gone through in my working life. You may feel unsatisfied with your job. You may feel unfulfilled. You may be trying to be someone you're not. My goal is to help you glean a better understanding of who you really are so that you can learn the one habit that leads to real happiness at work and guarantees success.

To me, being successful is not about how much money you make or how many people you influence; it's when you feel great about the work you do every day. If you absolutely love what you do and are challenged and fulfilled, you will maximize your true potential, feel like your work is making a real contribution, and have fun along the way. That's why I'm comfortable promising that success, however you define it, can be a given.

In my work as a performance strategist, I talk to all kinds of people who are grappling with the same questions that once kept me up at night. *What am I meant to do? What am I exceptional at?* I hear stories from people who are suffocating in support roles while their colleagues shoot right up the ladder or get to dive into the meaty work. These are people who have a sneaking suspicion that their potential is being wasted, but they don't know what to do or how to change.

Often my clients will blame themselves for feeling "off" in professional situations where, in fact, there's a real reason behind that sinking gut instinct. Whether it's anxiety about a stressful new role or assignment, a sense that the position their mentor recommended doesn't play to their strengths, or fear that they've strayed too far from their original career goals, many of the wildly different experiences of work dissatisfaction I hear about from my clients have a surprisingly similar root cause. Time and again, I've heard people describe the wide gulf between what they *want* to be doing—what they suspect is the wisest, most strategic, or most effective course of action or path forward—and what they have been told they *should* be doing.

I also hear from people who have just finished school and don't know where to start or have all but given up hope of finding work they could love. They wonder, *Isn't job dissatisfaction just another aspect of work?* Or, *You're not supposed to enjoy work. Just suck it up and do it.* And as for getting passed up for the promotion you really want or getting stuck doing thankless work instead of the more challenging stuff—well, who doesn't experience that at times?

My method, based on research by many leading thinkers in the fields of business, wellness, and psychology, shows not only that it is possible to find work that is deeply fulfilling and meaningful, but also that doing so is the secret sauce for attaining unlimited success and ongoing joy at work. In fact, fulfillment at work isn't just nice to have; it's the key to job security in a volatile, economically uncertain world. The way to get there is to figure out your *genius*—the thinking or problem-solving you do best, your purpose, the impact you have on others that fulfills you, and the core behaviors and thought patterns that are essential to great performance at work. It took me years to figure this out and then apply it precisely to my career, and my wish is that this book will help you get to the point of happiness and success faster than I did. If you apply these exercises and principles, you can make a significant shift in a short period of time.

I promise that you don't need to think like Albert Einstein to find and develop your genius. Genius is in each and every one of us; all you have to do is identify it within yourself and learn how to best apply it to your work every day. I hope the information in this book will help you gain clarity about who you are and where you're going, so you can proactively create the career of your dreams.

PART I

CHALLENGE

CHAPTER 1

YOU ARE ALREADY A GENIUS

Question: Are you bringing your unique thinking to work?

Genius Action Plan: Understand
the Genius Habit and Commit to the Process

You may have been taught that being a genius means you are exceptionally intelligent and can prove through your performance and aptitude that you are a singular talent, whether singing, leading a team, closing a deal, or performing surgery. Of course, the individual many people think of as being a genius is Einstein, but we have plenty of more recent public figures that many would consider to be geniuses as well. Steve Jobs was a genius in identifying why design matters in product development. Beyoncé is a musical and marketing genius for the unique way she launched her megaselling album *Lemonade*. George Lucas is a genius for creating the Star Wars universe. All these people have displayed outstanding aptitude and achievement in their fields, catapulting them to success that many of us only dream of, so we consider them to be geniuses.

While the dictionary's definition of *genius*—being an outstanding and unmatchable talent—is correct, I believe we need to start thinking about the concept of genius as something different and more accessible. What I have found, through my own career journey and my experience helping others find incredible success at work, is that everyone has a unique genius. Your genius is the distinctive way of thinking and problem-solving you already possess. It has more to do with *how* you approach work than the work itself. When you can access your genius at work, you'll find that it is a game changer: by understanding the way you work best and channeling that energy into your daily work, you will see that your job can become challenging in the best way possible, making it a joy instead of a chore.

In this book, you will learn that tapping into your genius is less about changing yourself and more about cultivating the gifts you already have into a highly effective way of operating. Rest assured that your genius is something you already engage with, whether or not you realize it. I'll help you identify your genius and understand how you can leverage it at work. Once you clearly define your genius and learn to nurture it, you can become exceptional at completing various tasks and processes—and use your genius in any number of ways to build a career that you find fulfilling.

One of my clients, for example, discovered her genius when she realized she felt most in the zone at work when she was coming up with new ideas and identifying the right language to make her ideas compelling to others. Because I believe it's useful to have a concrete phrase to define your genius, we crafted the name Content and Idea Architect to describe her innate strength. We created a strategy for increasing the amount of time she got to spend creating content at work. As a result of consciously identifying her genius and finding ways to incorporate it more often into her daily tasks, she immediately felt more engaged and confident with her job. Knowing the kind of work that most engaged her and yielded the best results gave her a deeper understanding of where her satisfaction and success should come from—and, best of all, she didn't need to go out and acquire new skills or try to change her innate tendencies. The answer to increased happiness and success at her job already lay within her.

Although the common definition of *genius* seems to imply that you either are one or you aren't, I have seen that your genius is not a fixed trait like IQ; it can be cultivated and improved over time. Humans' innate flexibility and ability to grow and develop is my proof that everyone is a genius in their own way; we just have to identify our strongest way of thinking, access it and apply it to new situations, and build a habit of accessing it in our daily lives. When you automatically seek out work that allows you to use your genius, you have attained a big part of the Genius Habit.

The Genius Habit

The Genius Habit comes from knowing how to bring the best aspects of your true self, along with other success-building behaviors, to work on a consistent basis. This habit ensures that you are always conscious of your performance and its direction. I've studied dozens of performance-improving frameworks and methods, many of which seemed useful, but I often found myself wondering whether it was possible that any of these methods could be applied to *any* person at *any* job. For me, what was missing from the performance strategies I was studying was an awareness of what was happening in the office day to day, at the granular level, and a way to clearly see how my decisions and behavior were connected to who I was as a person. I developed the Genius Habit to address those crucial elements, and I found that it improved my work performance and my morale, pushed me to dig deeper into who I was and how I worked best, and completely changed how I thought about work. Once I realized that the key to incredible performance was using my zone of genius to the point of habit, I knew I had stumbled across an idea that could help almost anyone be happier and more successful at work.

Humans unconsciously form habits as a shortcut, a way for the brain to be more efficient. According to Charles Duhigg, author of *The Power of Habit,* there is a simple neurological loop at the core of every habit.[1] The loop consists of three parts: a cue, a routine, and a reward. A cue is a signal that instructs your brain to start an automatic response that creates a physical, emotional, or mental routine, which leads to a reward. For example, I have a habit of drinking coffee in the morning. My cue is waking up and walking into the kitchen. The routine is brewing the coffee—measuring the coffee grounds and adding the water—all the while anticipating drinking it. The reward is the instant burst of energy I feel when I'm drinking a perfect hot cup. Because I engage in this sequence of activities every morning, I no longer have to think about each step of the process. Rather than hunting blindly for the coffee or my mug, my brain works on autopilot as I go through the motions of this habit loop.

Of course, some habits can be more complex than making coffee, and you may not even realize when you engage in habits at work, especially negative ones. Constantly checking your email when you should be focusing on productive work, for example, is a bad habit that has been widely studied and is notoriously difficult to break. Stopping by the kitchen every morning for a doughnut, staying at your desk for sad desk lunches every day, and gossiping with coworkers are other habits in the workplace that are easy to point to—but the concept can go much deeper. Sticking with the status quo because breaking out of it seems too difficult or overwhelming—such as is the case when you remain in a poorly

7

fitting job even though you know it's not right for you—can be viewed as a bad habit. In that case, the *cue* might be the feeling that something is not right: your work is boring, the constructive feedback you received in your last review is difficult to address, or you've lost your motivation. The *routine* occurs when you try to identify the reason for your negative feelings and blame the first thing that seems plausible: your manager, other colleagues, or some other external factor. The *reward*? You commiserate with your colleagues, and they validate your rationale; they may be equally frustrated or bored, and you are relieved that you are not alone in feeling this way. After all, isn't this just the way work has to be?

When you develop the bad habit of accepting and staying in a job that doesn't excite you, negative feelings toward work start to seem normal, and you accept these frustrations each time you commiserate with others who are in the same boat. When you're stuck in this loop, it may seem that changing jobs is the only way to break the habit of staying in a job you don't love, but the stress and bother of finding a new job may seem too daunting to tackle, so the bad habit continues.

The tendency to create bad habits can also occur on a broader career-planning level. The *cue* occurs when you start to feel that you're dissatisfied with your job and it may be time to move, but you don't know what new job you should pursue. The *routine* is looking for a new position and asking for advice from everyone you can think of, then blindly following it. The *reward* comes with the momentary relief of feeling less anxious because you have taken action based on the advice you received. The loop then begins again when you experience the same problems you faced at your previous job. Although you followed everyone's advice and went for an option that, on the surface, was an improvement, it eventually becomes clear that the new job isn't fun either and doesn't inspire you. This bad habit of changing jobs without truly understanding why you're dissatisfied or what will make you happier at work is one that many people face, and it contributes to the cultural belief that work can't and shouldn't be one of the best parts of your life.

If these scenarios sound familiar to you, it's time to build a new habit. I know that the people who love their jobs and are the most successful at work are the ones who use their zone of genius often and cultivate the right behaviors that allow them to grow and learn no matter what comes their way. When they experience the cue that something about their job is not quite working for them— whether they are bored or recognize that their performance is below their standards—they access a different routine that allows them to achieve an entirely different, more satisfying reward.

I'm going to give you the tools to break free of the bad habits you may have cultivated and look within yourself for the source of true happiness and success in your career. A tool I have developed, the Performance Tracker, is at the heart of this new routine. The Tracker provides questions to help you (1) understand what is at the root of your work problem and (2) help you identify what really matters to you as you navigate your career. You can also use the Tracker to help you determine what parts of your job you excel at, as well as proactively create more of those moments in your daily work. Once you understand your problems, you can fix them. By tracking your performance every week over the course of a few months, identifying when you are using your zone of genius, and engineering your daily work to better take advantage of your innate strengths and skills, you will be able to turn these processes and ways of thinking into a good habit that takes advantage of your brain's innate ability to create shortcuts and effortlessly allows you to be more successful at work. This is the Genius Habit.

By practicing the Genius Habit, you will find that the path to success is not as mysterious or as difficult as you might think. Happiness and job satisfaction are not about luck or good timing; they occur when you build a powerful habit that, week over week, creates the kind of success you have dreamed of achieving.

The idea of creating new habits can be daunting—after all, most of us have struggled to stick to a new exercise routine or diet plan. Understanding the process of habit formation can be an important step in setting yourself up for success. According to a study published in the *European Journal of Social Psychology*, researchers found that on average, it takes sixty-six days—a little more than two months—before a new behavior becomes automatic.[2] Breaking or creating a habit involves changing the neuronal, or cellular, connections in your brain. Every time you repeat a certain action, a specific neuronal pattern is stimulated and becomes strengthened. If you commit to following the exercises in this book and using the Performance Tracker weekly for sixty-six days, you'll be well on your way to creating the Genius Habit that will serve you for the rest of your life.

Once the Genius Habit becomes second nature, you will be better equipped to recognize and understand at any given moment why your work is boring. Or challenging. Or fulfilling. This understanding will give you an inner confidence and a deep knowledge that tapping into your unique zone of genius is the key to achieving whatever vision you see for yourself. You will be able to seamlessly adjust your work to align with your genius, create the impact that is fulfilling and navigate career changes with ease, and most importantly, achieve success faster than you previously expected. Most of all, using the Genius Habit will ensure that you love your work every day.

Meet the Performance Tracker: Your Genius Habit Tool

The main goal of the Performance Tracker is to help you know yourself more deeply. It is intended to help you understand the *how* of bringing the strongest aspects of yourself to your work every day and achieving the kind of success you want. In short, it keeps tabs on your progress with honing the Genius Habit. Think of the lessons in this book, combined with the Performance Tracker, as the guardrails on a highway. This information is meant to keep your career moving forward in a direction that's right for you. There are infinite ways in which you can be pulled off your path, but this methodology is meant to keep you on the right track and help you build the *routine* part of the habit loop that will make greatness at work a given.

I developed the Performance Tracker while working with clients to help them diagnose the root cause of their negative feelings about their work. I saw that they had difficulty identifying the underlying issues that were causing their problems. In my own experience, I had found that whenever I was bored in a corporate job and couldn't figure out why, instead of looking within myself, I would blame the most obvious external reason: it was my manager's fault, or the company was limiting me, or my coworkers were a pain. But once I started tracking the details of my work week after week, it allowed me more insight into my own performance. I saw that problems often were coming from within myself, or from the fact that certain aspects of my work didn't inherently match up with my best assets. The information I recorded in the tracker was the key to knowing when to pivot or to focus more intently. Now, I help my clients use the Performance Tracker to ensure that when things at work aren't going well, they can more easily identify the root cause, change their behavior, and get a better result.

What I love about this tool is its simplicity. It requires only ten to fifteen minutes each week. You'll answer a series of simple questions that are a distillation of the most recent discoveries in psychology and the science of performance. Your answers will allow you to see the reality of what's going on in your work life, so it's important to answer each question as honestly and specifically as possible. After filling out the Tracker, you are assigned a score, which you can compare week to week to track your progress.

Many of my clients report that this simple act of tracking has brought them profound insights about behaviors and patterns they didn't know were at the root of their frustrations. When the Performance Tracker is used regularly, I have seen it help my clients gain an increased understanding of themselves, a deeper awareness of what's holding them back, and clarity on what they need to do to move their careers forward. I continue to use the Tracker myself, and it has helped me quickly diagnose issues I encounter, course-correct when necessary, and have more control of my career destiny.

You'll also find that the Tracker is one of the best ways to prepare you for your company's review process. Most businesses still operate under an outdated performance model, in which your success at work is evaluated by others—likely your supervisor and perhaps other colleagues. Like most people, if you receive a positive evaluation, you likely don't question your efforts or strive to make significant changes. Why would you? It's only when things go wrong or you receive negative feedback that you might start thinking about the big picture or attempt deep self-reflection.

If you're honing your Genius Habit, you don't have to wait for a performance review to figure out whether you are successful. You'll be in a constant state of evaluation, knowing that using your zone of genius is the best way to get tasks done and determine what new areas you should explore if you are unhappy or floundering in a job that doesn't feel right. You can learn how to identify the type of work that is personally satisfying and presents just the right amount of challenge to keep you hungry and motivated. You will use that knowledge to leap ahead in your career.

You can access the Performance Tracker at the end of this book. For best results, fill it out every week for a few months. By doing so you will see patterns in your performance emerge and gain the knowledge to more powerfully take the reins of your daily work experience.

FORGET ABOUT YOUR IQ

If you are a rocket scientist, your genius might be in the way you gather data and solve big problems, which requires the use of your awesome math and physics skills and off-the-charts IQ.

If you aren't a rocket scientist, it doesn't mean you are not a genius! While a high IQ is a sign of intelligence, our understanding of its importance as an indicator of success has changed dramatically over the past few decades. Historically, IQ has been considered a fixed element of potential success, but we now know that IQ is a variable that can actually be increased by focused effort. Some of the activities associated with increasing your IQ include stepping outside of your comfort zone, building your relational skills, enriching your language, eating healthy food, and exercising vigorously.[3] This means that IQ is not some sort of guarantee of professional success, or lack thereof. In fact, the act of tackling IQ-enhancing practices, and sticking to them, says more about your likelihood for success than your IQ itself.

More importantly, the idea that IQ is the only indicator of future achievement has been completely debunked. Martin Seligman's work in positive psychology has shown a clear link between positive thinking and success,[4] while Carol Dweck's research on the growth mind-set—the understanding that intelligence and skill can grow over time—has become the bible for forward-thinking people and companies. Later in this book, you'll read about some of their most surprising insights, which turn some of our most deeply held beliefs about performance, motivation, and success on their heads.

It's Not about Doing What You Love; It's about Doing What You Are Meant to Do

The methodology I share in these pages has brought me—and many of my high-profile clients—closer to work that is exciting and meaningful every day. We feel a newfound sense of confidence in our skills and less fear about the future. We recognize that while there are a host of variables we cannot control—swift shifts in the technological landscape, uncertainties in our industries, and instability in the economy as a whole—we stand firm in our understanding of our innate abilities and, ultimately, our purpose.

Given everything that's been written about purpose, the act of identifying it may seem like an overwhelming task—*purpose* is, after all, a loaded word that means different things to different people. Is it doing work with a charitable or social justice component? Is it finding work that's fun? Does purposeful work need to be meaningful?

The good news is that you can stop searching far and wide for your purpose because you already have it—you just need to get in touch with it. Purposeful work is simply work that you find fulfilling. It is work that's connected to what I call your *core emotional challenge*—a struggle you overcame at some point in your life or an issue you continue to struggle with. If you can identify your core emotional challenge, invariably you will find fulfillment by helping others with this same core challenge.

My clients often find that their core emotional challenge isn't just one moment of difficulty they experienced, but rather a pattern that appears throughout their lives. My core emotional challenge, for example, is not being seen. Growing up, I always felt different from the rest of my family, as if nobody truly understood who I was. This core emotional challenge has followed me throughout life. I get the most upset when I feel that I am not being seen or my words and opinions are not being taken seriously. Also, I have found that the work that is most fulfilling to me relates to addressing this same core emotional challenge in others—helping others see themselves and be seen clearly by others.

You might be already tapping into this source of motivation within yourself—you just may not know it. I'll share questions, techniques, and stories to help you clearly identify your purpose and core emotional challenge. You'll use this information to create an action plan to maximize the time you spend doing work that you find meaningful, fulfilling, and fun. By marrying this knowledge with your genius, you'll be able to know yourself on a whole new level, and you'll also be able to identify the work that really excites you. I refer to this overlap—the work that both uses your genius and fulfills your purpose—as operating in your "Zone of Genius."

Genius Action Plan: Understand the Genius Habit and Commit to the Process

I came up with the Zone of Genius model when I discovered how effective it was in my own transition from struggling at work to finding incredible fulfillment. Identifying my genius and purpose and using them in tandem as a lens for making career decisions was a major breakthrough for me, and I've seen my clients use it to reach similar success. In this book you're going to learn the five core performance principles necessary for effectively operating within your Zone of Genius and creating the success you want—Challenge, Impact, Joy, Mindfulness, and Perseverance—and the behaviors that accompany them. The Genius Habit is the ability to automatically apply these principles and behaviors to your job while working within your Zone of Genius.

Challenge: Early on in my journey of seeking the secrets to fulfillment at work, reading Mihaly Csikszentmihalyi's seminal book *Flow* catalyzed my thinking on performance. In the book, he argues that a key ingredient for attaining the flow state is creating work that provides just the right amount of challenge. I have since observed that most of my clients who are unhappy at work misdiagnose their situation by blaming the job, the manager, or the organization. In fact, their struggles often boil down to a lack of personal challenge.

Impact: Many companies think that if they provide free lunch, massages, and game rooms, their employees will be more motivated. But as social scientist Alfie Kohn observed, such perks do little to change people's attitudes about their jobs.[5] What *does* lead to motivation is having a better understanding of the impact of your work. Adam Grant, professor at the Wharton School at

University of Pennsylvania, found that lifeguards who read about their ability to avert fatalities—and therefore understood the impact of their work—increased their work hours by more than 40 percent, while those who merely learned that a lifeguard gig could be personally enriching kept working at the same rate.[6]

Clearly, understanding your impact on others is important, but I have found that when you can identify an impact that is specifically meaningful and is connected to your core emotional challenge, that is when you begin to fulfill your purpose. The truth is, we all operate from our purpose, and we do it often; we just don't notice when we do. My client Jane was known in her office for her extreme generosity, but it wasn't until we started working together that she realized the significance of her generosity. When we dug deeper, Jane realized that she had a core emotional challenge attached to this behavior that she previously hadn't been aware of. Once we identified the cause and understood why this behavior was so fulfilling to her, we strategized about how she could create more opportunities to be generous at work and ultimately feel more fulfilled by her job.

Joy: Time and time again, I have seen that most people who *think* they like their work are actually "achievement junkies" like I was, addicted to the dopamine hit they get every time they meet a goal or receive external validation. They don't realize that when much of their satisfaction at work comes from reaching goals—big salaries, coveted promotions, impressive titles—they're missing out on the energizing, everyday sense of joy they could get from a job that's aligned with their genius and purpose. Achievement junkies often suffer from burnout, anxiety, and the never-ending stress of chasing another challenge. If your goal is to find joy at work, which path seems better to you?

There are many advantages to finding authentic joy at work. A 2015 study by economists at the University of Warwick found that happiness at work led to a 12 percent spike in productivity, while unhappy workers proved 10 percent less productive. As the research team put it, "We find that human happiness has large and positive causal effects on productivity. Positive emotions appear to invigorate human beings."[7] In other words, authentic fulfillment serves as a bulletproof vest at work; it deflects stress and helps you push the boundaries of your comfort zone, tackle setbacks with ease, and enjoy working as a team player.

Mindfulness: Drawing on more than one hundred interviews, a pilot study at the University of Melbourne found a clear correlation between high levels of confidence and occupational success.[8] We all instinctively know that confident people tend to be more successful, but how exactly does one create confidence? When I was beginning my journey to create a career that I loved, I searched far and wide for a framework to help me understand the daily habits I needed to cultivate in order to manage my own career success and performance, but I came up empty-handed. So I built my own framework. My confidence soared, erasing the negative thoughts I had suffered previously. In addition, incorporating Carol Dweck's research on building a growth mind-set into the process of building the Genius Habit is another essential building block for confidence.

We all have negative mental chatter, yet few of us are aware of its power over our thinking and behavior and ultimately our career potential. I have found that adopting mindfulness techniques—which allow you to instantly pinpoint the reason you are feeling anxious, stressed, or unsure at work—is one of the best ways to hone the Genius Habit. Throughout the book we will use mindfulness in a number of ways to identify and define your genius, as well as find and eliminate self-sabotaging behaviors.

Perseverance: We are taught from a young age that disappointments and failures are something we should be ashamed of. We think they reflect badly on our potential, but the truth about failure is quite the opposite. Failures are often our greatest teachers and make us stronger. Overcoming setbacks requires perseverance, and when it comes to adopting the Genius Habit, knowing what makes you stronger allows you to see failures as opportunities.

Research on the power of resiliency and grit, combined with curiosity, shows that perseverance pays dividends over IQ. We all have the opportunity to cultivate grit, especially in the face of adversity, but it takes discipline and awareness to do so. Cultivating the Genius Habit is all about tracking your behaviors around growth and becoming more resilient so that you can turn these concepts into concrete ways of thinking and behaving when facing challenges in your work.

The New Skill You Need to Learn

Parallel to my own personal journey, the business world has been shifting. With the process of traditional performance reviews becoming obsolete, automation increasing, and businesses needing fresh ideas and rapid innovation, there has never been more of a need for individuals to learn the skills of motivating themselves and managing their own performance. According to the McKinsey Global Institute Report *Jobs Lost, Jobs Gained: Workforce Transitions in a Time of Automation*, by 2030, "Activities within all occupations will shift. New work will involve more application of expertise, interaction, and management. In addition, future work activities will require more social emotional, creative, and logical reasoning abilities."[9]

Let's Get Started

If you are truly committed to making a change in your career, it won't take long to permanently transform your work life and become your most efficient, confident, and joyful self. Once you're operating in your Zone of Genius, all the energy that has been swirling around as you search to find your "thing" will become refocused toward your work and your mission. By uncovering, articulating, and using your gifts, you will be known and remembered for exactly who you are and what you have to offer this world.

My hope is that after reading this book you will be ready for work that lights you up and that the sheer act of questioning yourself and tapping into your Zone of Genius triggers others you know to do the same. When I'm around people who are doing what they love to do, I'm inspired, and the world needs more inspired and inspiring people who are willing to take on challenging but infinitely rewarding work. Let's begin!

CHAPTER 2

IF YOU'RE FAILING AT YOUR JOB, YOU'RE IN THE WRONG JOB

Question: Is your job challenging or boring?

Genius Action Plan: Determine if
You're in the Right Job

An Ivy League graduate who's ready to flee his six-figure salary to open a dog rescue center. A promising young film producer who can't understand why she's failing at even the most basic administrative tasks. An up-and-coming CEO who can no longer make it through a meeting without an anxiety attack. What do these people have in common?

Like most of my clients, they each came to me with a long list of reasons why they were failing at their jobs. Each was convinced that they either needed to up their game—work harder, gain a new skill, or better motivate themselves—or escape their industry altogether. And each was grappling with big questions about their worth, their future career plans, and their ability to succeed while getting more enjoyment from work.

In my experience, most performance problems are related to a poor job fit. If you've ever been fired or received a poor performance review, you know the message HR usually sends is that you are not a good fit for the position. Yet they say it in a misleading way, such as, "Here are the areas you need to develop in order to succeed in this job." The message there is that you need to change, be different. Most people hear those words as, "I'm not good enough the way I am. I need to work on these development areas."

When we're feeling uneasy at work, the default solution often is to try to become what we think our organization or industry wants us to be. This tactic seems rational, but I have found over and over again that it leads us deeper down the road to dissatisfaction and its cousin misery.

If you feel your job is boring, anxiety-inducing, or overwhelming, I have good news for you: It's not you; it's your job. Boredom is one of the early warning signs that you're not fully engaged or appropriately challenged, and stress and burnout are signals that you've been stuck in the wrong role for much too long. If you're feeling unhappy, unchallenged, or unfulfilled, those are clues that something about your current situation is not allowing you to use your genius—the unique problem-solving ability that makes you *you*.

The next time you hear those disappointing words from HR, instead of thinking about what you've done wrong, think about how you can find work that is more aligned with the real you. You might think, *Wait a second, the abilities I lack are not connected to my strengths, and they are likely not something that I can ever master. This is probably a no-win situation for me. Thanks for allowing me the opportunity to figure out this part of my work life.*

Finding the job that's uniquely suited to your skills and values is possible, but it's not something that can be left to luck. It's also not something that your mentor or manager or therapist or mother can figure out for you. It requires you to be proactive and learn about a subject you might have never studied before: *you*. Because the truth is you can achieve success and greatness by being who you are if you are strategic with your special skills and assets, and if you are willing to build the habits essential for great performance.

While children are legally required to spend a minimum of twelve years in the classroom, unless you were lucky enough to have attended a highly evolved educational program, you've probably never been encouraged to get to know yourself all that well. And while therapy and coaching are growing more popular, the stigma remains that they are expensive resources to turn to only when something's wrong in your life, not tools to use to maximize your potential. What's more, many people hold fast to antiquated ideas about work in general. *If you can't stay focused at work, it's because there's something wrong with you. If you find a particular task difficult, it's because you're incompetent or lazy.* Some people will become so demoralized that they will give up on a company or industry long before they have had a chance to diagnose the real problem, and they will likely find themselves back in the same situation in a few years. Others will start working long hours to overcompensate for what they perceive to be a lack of skill or competence. This obviously can create even more anxiety about job performance.

This book is meant to help you figure out who you are, including your unique skills and underlying motivations, and to help you recognize when you're working in your Zone of Genius. You're in your Zone of Genius when you're able to apply your genius to your work while making the impact that's most meaningful to you. By identifying your Zone of Genius and adjusting your work so that it revolves around your genius and purpose, you avoid the feelings of confusion and anxiety about work that many people can't escape.

Before we further explore the concepts of genius and purpose, let's first figure out how things are going for you at work right now. If you're like most people, I bet you have at least a small amount of anxiety about your next performance review and what your manager might say about your work. For now, let's worry less about what your manager thinks and focus more on what you think.

It took me a long time to ask myself the right question: *Am I in the wrong job?* Or, to be more precise: *Does my job provide the right kind of challenge for me?*

Using Your Genius Makes Hard Work Energizing

The right kind of work challenges should be hard—but in a good way. These challenges occur when you are thinking, processing, and problem-solving a specific task. You know that you're capable of coming up with the right answers; you just haven't figured out all the pieces yet. There's a positive energy about this challenge: you're looking forward to solving the problem and getting the right outcome. What feels exciting and energizing to you is that tension between knowing what you can do and wondering how you will exactly do it.

Mihaly Csikszentmihalyi, the pioneering psychologist and the author of the groundbreaking book *Flow*, has his own definition for this kind of challenge: "The best moments usually occur if a person's body or mind is stretched to its limits in a voluntary effort to accomplish something difficult and worthwhile." In other words, we are most engaged when we are doing work that pushes us beyond our comfort zone yet isn't so stressful that it inhibits enjoyment.

Csikszentmihalyi uses this definition to describe *flow*: when you're in flow, you're so immersed in what you're doing that you lose track of time. You feel confident and the work is invigorating. In fact, Csikszentmihalyi's research found that people are happiest when they're working, as long as the work is something they enjoy and is sufficiently challenging.

Csikszentmihalyi defines challenging work, or flow, as meeting three criteria:

1. *The work must contain a goal that you can measure yourself against*: For me, this refers to the ability to see progression and a specific outcome.

2. *You need to have feedback on that goal*: You should seek out valid confirmation that your goal has been achieved.

3. *One must have a good balance between the perceived challenges of the task and their own perceived skills*: This is what I call the sweet spot of challenge.

When I first read Csikszentmihalyi's definition of flow, what stood out for me was that most people are meeting the first two criteria: they are setting goals and getting feedback. But most people don't know how to best access the third part of the equation. Without an understanding of how the challenge of your work matches up with your skills, you may be left wondering how to manage a performance problem or how to attain performance success.

The Myth of Blissful Retirement

We can't really blame people for settling for jobs they don't really love. After all, popular wisdom holds that work is something to be begrudgingly endured for a few decades before the bliss of retirement. In fact, we're taught that a life of leisure—lazy days sitting on the beach, sipping piña coladas, or spending time not working—is the ultimate joy. When you think about what it would be like to win the lottery, do you really envision yourself going back to work? After all, we think that people who don't have to work are the luckiest.

But research tells us otherwise: as Csikszentmihalyi observed, we are actually happiest when we are working, but that requires doing work that you gets you in the zone. And along with being happier, we're also healthier. A 2016 study from Oregon State University found that healthy adults who retired just one year past age sixty-five had an 11 percent lower risk of death from all causes compared to those who retired at sixty-five (the study factored in demographic, lifestyle, and health issues).[10] If you enjoy your work enough to keep at it, the happiness it brings may very well increase your longevity.

Similar to the messages we've all heard about how we should work hard now in order to enjoy retirement later, we are equally inundated with messages about success. *You have to work hard to get ahead. A high salary and good benefits are more important than joy. You need a laundry list of credentials before you're considered an expert.*

We accept these messages as truth because our brains are wired to conform to the thinking of the crowd. Psychologist Solomon Asch conducted an experiment in the 1950s that crystallized his research on groupthink.[11] His experiments featured groups of people making basic decisions about whether a set of lines matched in size. He planted actors in the room to purposely give false answers and found that when the majority of people gave a particular answer (even if it was false), the unaware person went along with the group. This connection to conformity and avoidance of conflict is so deeply entrenched in the brain that we react to disagreements in a similar manner to punishment.[12] This is one powerful reason why it is so difficult to go against the groupthink of what work is supposed to look and feel like and stay steadfast in your belief that it should be fun. It's much easier to follow the lead of those around us, conform, and stay in a job we don't love. This is also why outside-the-box thinking is a rebellious act of stepping out of your comfort zone, and why creating a new kind of work that you'll love requires being a maverick. I know from personal experience that when I started creating my dream job, I had zero validation from society, and my family didn't understand what I was doing. Staying in a job that wasn't ideal for me was a much more understandable and accepted norm. And that goes hand in hand with rethinking what your own retirement will look like. Personally, I'm not working toward the standard-issue retirement plan; I want to do the work that I love as long as I am mentally capable and save the relaxation for vacations. Your idea of retirement may be different from mine, but I would encourage you not to accept the myth of blissful retirement and seek fulfillment from your job now, rather than grinding it out for the next twenty years.

My experience working with hundreds of clients at all levels of their careers bears this theory out: the people I meet who are the least challenged are often the most frustrated and depressed. I have struggled with depression at times, especially when I was unhappy at work, including a severe bout when I was living at my parents' home and waiting tables. Now I understand that my depression was largely driven by the disconnect between my high ambition and my less-challenging job that had no prospect of advancement. I was in a state of absolute confusion: waiting tables was not what I wanted to be doing. It didn't provide the type of challenge I needed in order to thrive, but I didn't know what else to do. I didn't fully understand that part of my frustration was linked to my inability to see myself for who I was and link that to the opportunities that would be the right fit for me.

If you're dreaming of quitting everything and moving to a deserted island, the next set of questions will help you identify whether that dream is grounded in a true longing for a lifestyle shift—and that may well be the case—or the result of fatigue due to a poor work fit. If, on the other hand, you're not quite ready to turn in your company ID but you do have a sense that your job could be a lot more rewarding, rest assured that more fulfilling work is well within your grasp.

Genius Action Plan: Determine If You're in the Right Job

Your job should feel like it is a good fit for you and provide the right amount of challenge. The next two exercises are meant to help you figure out both.

Is Your Job a Good Fit for You?

To see if your job is the right fit, answer yes or no to the following questions:

1. When you get constructive feedback, does it often require you to work on a skill or ability that doesn't feel intuitive to you?

   YES
   NO

2. Do coworkers who are moving up the ladder quickly have a vastly different skill set from you?

   YES
   NO

3. Do you often feel insecure because no matter how hard you work you still can't seem to meet expectations?

   YES
   NO

4. Does becoming a superstar employee at your company or job seem impossible?

   YES
   NO

5. Does work mostly feel like drudgery, like the clock is ticking too slowly rather than the day speeding by?

   YES
   NO

6. Does your manager struggle to "get" you?

   YES
   NO

7. Do you have a continual "off" feeling at work, but you can't pinpoint why?

   YES
   NO

8. Is job security or benefits one of the main reasons you stay at your company?   **YES** **NO**

9. Do you feel that looking for a new job is scarier than dealing with the day-to-day tasks of your current role?   **YES** **NO**

10. Do you often wonder if feeling mediocre at work is as good as it gets?   **YES** **NO**

If you answered yes to six or more questions: You definitely are in the wrong job. But guess what? You should be celebrating. Why? Because you probably thought you weren't good enough at what you do, and that's absolutely not the case. Being in a job that isn't meant for you is like wearing clothes that aren't the right size; you'll never be able to make it work.

Working at the wrong job is something you can change. Now that you know your job isn't the right fit, your path forward is a lot clearer than it might have been just an hour ago. But don't hand in your letter of resignation yet: first, we'll figure out what your perfect challenge looks like. By the end of this book you'll have much more clarity about where you want to go.

If you answered yes to three to five questions: You're probably in a job that is not quite ideal for you. Maybe you've found a decent balance of tasks you love and those you can't stand. But if you're still answering yes to many of these questions over the next three months, you will know it's probably time to move on.

Even if that happens, take heart. You're paying attention to what's right and wrong with your job fit. That is a huge step forward in the direction of finding work you love. The Performance Tracker will be an incredibly useful tool for you as it gives you deeper insight into the kinds of tasks and responsibility that you like best—and the ones that leave you staring out the window longing for the day to end.

If you answered yes to two or fewer questions: Great news: you're in a job that seems like a great fit! But that doesn't mean you can't get value from this book. You're going to walk away with tools to take more ownership over the direction of your career and an understanding of how to advocate for the work that is right for you. If you already have the freedom to direct some of your tasks, you're in a great position to increase the amount of time you spend operating in your Zone of Genius.

Does Your Job Provide the Right Kind of Challenge?

GOOD CHALLENGE

1. When you're working, do you enjoy the thinking process that it involves?

   YES
   NO

2. Even if the volume of work is more than you can handle, do you still enjoy doing the work?

   YES
   NO

BAD CHALLENGE

1. Are you are overwhelmed by the amount of work you have and the effort it will take to do it?

   YES
   NO

2. Are you bored and unmotivated, letting work pile up until you are left with an unmanageable load?

   YES
   NO

If you answered one or two yeses in the Good Challenge section, you are in a job that provides the right kind of challenge. If you had one or two yeses in the Bad Challenge section, it's probable that the work you're doing is most likely not in the sweet spot of challenge for you.

By reviewing the answers to the previous questions, you should now have a sense of how good a fit your current job is and if you're being challenged in the right way. If you're like many of my clients, you may be feeling a sense of relief knowing that your feeling of discontent isn't a sign of incompetence, but rather a signal that you need to make a change.

Changing Jobs Doesn't Mean Defeat

The fear of change keeps many of my clients in jobs that are clearly not the right fit. In fact, it's quite common for me to run across highly successful senior executives that acknowledge the wrongness of their jobs but don't proactively pursue change.

Jim was a senior executive in a company of 35,000 employees who ran a department of 350 people. There were definitely things he liked about his job, including the company culture and his colleagues. But he also had to grudgingly accept the long hours that kept him anxious and away from his family. What's more, he didn't love the tasks he spent most of the day addressing. He had been hired to do a job that, on paper, he was well qualified for. But after a few months the job evolved to being more operational and less visionary, and he didn't have the skills that were required to do the work well. He kept trying to prove that he could excel at the execution but ran up against hurdle after hurdle, making his job feel more like a burden than a joy.

Even though he was aware that he was being forced to work in ways that weren't intuitive to him, Jim resisted the idea of change or leaving the company. Everyone in his industry held this company in high regard, and he really admired his superiors. Change, in his mind, meant defeat. Instead, he reached out to me, hoping I could teach him the skills to succeed in his current position.

The first step was to determine if the job was a good fit, and we quickly realized it wasn't. I explained to Jim that when a job presents challenges that aren't aligned with your genius and your purpose, it will always take you twice as long to accomplish your tasks. You could end up getting it right eventually, but the effort would be inefficient and mentally exhausting. The gap between the job's required skills and Jim's strengths might have been one of the reasons he had to stay so late at work to get everything accomplished. If Jim had been tackling challenges that were the right fit for his skills and that he found exciting, he would likely have conquered them faster. He also would have felt good about his work and would have gotten better results.

Jim understood that the operational challenges he was presented with were difficult, but because they weren't interesting to him, they seemed frustratingly complex and tiring to solve. I suggested that if he really wanted to stay at this company, he needed to hire someone to oversee the operational parts of the job so he could stick to what he was good at, which was the visionary work. Jim agreed with the strategy. Once he created the right team to support him, he would be able to get back into the zone of the big-picture work he really enjoyed.

However, I still didn't think that Jim was in the right job. His genius of being a visionary aligned more with consulting than working for just one company for the long haul. He agreed and began looking for a new job that would offer the right challenges he could get excited about. Unfortunately, the next job he took was very similar to the one he left.

Today, Jim is still unhappy; his new company's culture is even more operationally minded, and the challenges he's presented with still don't energize him. He's attracted to these jobs because of the prestige that is attached, and he fails to recognize how much of the role requires mastering his weaknesses rather than using his genius. He couldn't shake the feeling that in order to be successful he needed to build his abilities within his areas of weakness.

I share this story because Jim is no different from many others I have met. The fact that his job was challenging him in a way that felt burdensome was nothing new—he had been taught that is what work was supposed to feel like. Even today, he has difficulty accepting that work challenges can be stimulating instead of frustrating, and that he can be successful without having to master work that he isn't naturally good at.

What Kind of Work Are You Ready For?

Here are three more questions to think about—and the answers aren't ones that can be tracked or quantified. These are the kinds of questions that might reveal your hidden biases, hopes, and fears about work. So much of knowing yourself better involves letting go of what others have told you about achievement and success—and learning to trust that you already have all the answers inside.

What's Your Version of Success?

What is your definition of work?

_____

_____

_____

_____

_____

_____

What is your definition of success?

_____

_____

_____

_____

_____

_____

What is your current vision for your career?

_____

_____

_____

_____

_____

_____

When I ask myself these questions, I define work as a part of my life that I delight in and that is always a source of challenge and fulfillment. To me, success is spending the majority of my time on work or tasks that are fulfilling, leveraging my Zone of Genius, maximizing my potential, and helping other people in a meaningful way while providing the freedom, lifestyle, and experiences I desire. My vision for my career is always expanding. At the moment, my vision is to help thousands of people see themselves for who they are and build habits that allow them to maximize their joy and fulfillment at work.

Are you struggling to define success for yourself? Here are some responses from people I've interviewed. See if any of their language resonates with you and helps you build your own definitions.

"To find and fully live your purpose in life, and to leave an enduring legacy of having made a difference in the world."

—Ron Cordes, cofounder of the Cordes Foundation

"I define success as living my true purpose and having a positive impact on the lives of people by uplifting them and inspiring them to think and act in ways that they may not have considered before."

—Raj Sisodia, cofounder of Conscious Capitalism and professor at Babson College

"The purpose of our lives is to contribute our unique,
God-given gifts to have an extraordinary positive
impact on the lives of others and the world."
—**David S. Kidder, cofounder and CEO of Bionic**

"Success, for me, has always been in providing a
great quality of life for my family, for those who
work for me, and to my community."
—**Jeremy Young, CEO of Tanga**

"My definition of success is knowing that what you are doing is
helping you and others lead a better, happier, healthier life."
—**Kara Goldin, founder and CEO of Hint Water**

"To me, success means creating a business that
empowers customers, employees, and community in
equal measure. We want to add positive value to people's
lives, from a personal and professional standpoint."
—**Dan Kurzius, cofounder and COO of MailChimp**

"Success is looking back at your life, when you are in your
final moments, and possessing a great amount of pride
around your creations, accomplishments, and legacy, while
possessing little to no regret about what you did not do

and missed opportunities (i.e., your family still loves you). If I can die feeling this way, I believe this is success."

—Seth Besmertnik, CEO of Conductor

"I feel that my life is successful if I can live each day with a positive outlook, have a feeling of contentment with my circumstances, have balance in all the important areas of my life, and have the time and resources to pursue what I am passionate about."

—Marcia Becker, PhD, senior director of Adult Rehabilitative and Rural Services (my mom)

"I define success as having a job that you enjoy and enables you financially, a spouse and family that loves and cares for you, children that make you proud by who they are and what they do, having the freedom to worship a loving God, and being able to contribute to the betterment of your fellow man. I am so blessed!"

—E. N. Garnett Jr., Certified Crop Advisor, Southern States (my dad)

YOU CAN MASTER THE RIGHT KIND OF CHALLENGES

Trust that if you plow forward, practice will help you get comfortable with knowing when something is the right challenge, meaning it's not too hard and it's not too easy. You'll learn to harness that nervous energy so it drives you forward.

- If you're drawn to speaking yet getting up on stage scares you, trust in your desire and know that you can overcome your fear through practice. Start small—organize a mini-event with a few trusted friends or consider a class at your local theater or improv school. Or join Toastmasters to help get you out of your comfort zone.

- If there is a project you are dying to manage yet the thought of it also creates a nervous feeling in your stomach, go for it anyway. Use that nervous energy toward research and learning to help you feel up to the challenge of tackling something new. Ask your colleagues or manager for feedback as you approach uncharted territory; their feedback can help you analyze your impact and make sure you are having the impact that is right for you.

- If you know you're meant to write a book but you're not sure on the topic, start small and work your way up to a longer form. You can write blogs or articles or post messages on social media with your ideas. Let your genius and purpose guide your choice of content.

The Next Step

Now, let's get started identifying your genius. If you've ever wondered what makes your experience and expertise special, why you're the one for the job, or how you could squeeze more enjoyment out of the time you spend at work, it's time to start asking the right questions and figure out how you like to work.

CHAPTER 3

IDENTIFYING YOUR GENIUS

Question: When are you in the zone at work?

Genius Action Plan: Identify How You
Like to Think at Work Now

When I sign on a new client, one of the first things many ask me is, "My credentials are top-notch, I've worked for the best companies, and I have a good job...so why am I miserable?" Every time, I tell them that happiness cannot be found in a single job, and it doesn't always come with a bigger paycheck. My goal is to show them that while happiness may seem to be dependent on external factors, it actually comes from within. When you like who you are, whether it's at work or in your personal life, you'll be happy.

Humans have an innate tendency to dream about future possibilities instead of enjoying the present. According to Daniel Gilbert, bestselling author of *Stumbling on Happiness*, our brains are programmed to anticipate what is coming and prepare for the future. The upside of this is that we can speculate about what we think will make us happy. The downside is that those dreams can become obsessions or unfulfilled wishes. When we say to ourselves, *I'd be so much happier if I was richer or skinnier or in a different job*, our powerful prefrontal cortex, the thinking center of the brain that pulls information from our memories, allows us to create a vision of what life would be like if only we could meet those goals. When we see that perfection in our minds and compare it to where we are or what we are doing, the difference between our reality and dreams leads to unhappiness.

Unfortunately, our visions of the future have no validity. Just because we can imagine our future selves does not necessarily mean that the outcome would align with our expectations. And even if we were to get the thing we think we want—the new job, the bigger paycheck, the important client—there's no guarantee that it would make us happy. At best, reaching that goal might create a momentary positive blip before we go back to our normal state of happiness (or unhappiness).[13]

The real question, then, is not whether you are happy at work. Instead, let's figure out if you are actively challenged in a way that excites you intellectually. Are you working to your highest potential? Are you engaging with the right kind of tasks? And most importantly, do you have the opportunity to shine, staying true to your authentic self?

Your genius is the way you process information that is most enjoyable and effective for you. When you're using your genius at work, time flies. It's a visceral feeling that many people describe as being in the zone—fully engaged and challenged in a way that is not too easy or too hard. You're heavily immersed in your work and not bothered by distractions. You're challenged but not overwhelmed. You're excited, and you feel a sense of confidence and accomplishment. You feel as though you're on fire.

My client Steve finds that he is most challenged when he is having informative conversations with a variety of people, understanding their opinions and ideas, then creating one cohesive strategy that addresses all their needs. The process of collaborating and pulling all the ideas into one concept is his favorite and most effective method of working, so we named his genius Collaboration Strategist.

Another client, Sarah, learned that she is best suited for working on projects that require thinking outside the box and seeing beyond the conventional wisdom. She is in the zone when she is creating new ways of thinking and leading a team to execute on that new idea. In her job, she enjoys reinventing how a particular department operates and redesigning how products are developed and brought to market. She now refers to her genius as a Barrier-Breaking Visionary.

I spend a lot of time talking with my clients about when they are in the zone. I help them pinpoint what that unique process is, I put a name to it, and I help them notice when they're using it and when they're not. I've also found that once you identify the thinking that is most exciting to you, you can actually hone in on it and figure out how to use that type of thinking more often.

While it's tempting to revert to thinking about genius in the traditional sense, my version has nothing to do with the grades you got in school. Your genius does, however, define your go-to way of processing information. Some people's genius may have contributed to them getting good grades. For others, their go-to way of thinking wasn't one that was useful in completing school-work and may have actually worked against them in school. Some of my more creative and successful clients excel in settings that are far removed from book learning. To them, the classroom always felt boring, and as a result they struggled to remain engaged or perform at a high level in school.

Conversely, just because you did well in school does not mean you're going to kill it in the work world. Academic settings often require memorization, and if you happen to have a photo-graphic memory, you may have gotten straight As in the classes that required you to read and regurgitate information. When you entered the workforce, however, you may have been shocked when your first job had nothing to do with memorization. You may have failed because you were so used to relying on those abilities that operating in a world that requires unique problem-solving and execution may have been overwhelming.

This idea of using your unique genius to attain excellence has been missing in the literature and cultural attitudes about career success, which tend to focus on more basic characteristics that have been universally accepted as positive and effective. Performing well on standardized tests, getting good grades, and being outgoing are traits often considered inherent to success. But the skills needed to thrive in a career go well beyond what is traditionally taught in school or valued by society.

One of the keys to success in the business world is innovation, which calls for creativity, problem-solving, and thinking outside the box—not necessarily skills you're encouraged to develop in today's educational environment. Being creative and solving problems that have no obvious solution by thinking in a visionary way requires a deep belief in yourself and an appreciation for your value. The only way to cultivate this ability is to know yourself, understand your genius, and leverage it for your career. When you are trying to uncover your genius, you've got to reexamine your past successes and failures inside the school system and at previous jobs. You need to think about every aspect of your life.

Genius Action Plan: Identify How You Like to Think at Work Now

The first step to identifying your genius is to find the places in your job where you already use it. Let's pinpoint the moments when you feel in the zone. Ask yourself the following questions. Resist the urge to say the "right" thing or the smart thing, the thing you think your manager wants to hear, or the thing you think will bring you the most recognition and accolades.

1. What are the moments and what are the tasks I am doing when I am in the zone at work? These are the times where I'm intellectually on fire, stimulated, and feel like my work is important.

2. What is the type of thinking or problem-solving that caused this feeling?

3. When am I clearly out of the zone—bored, distracted, frustrated?

Next, think about three work projects you have completed during which you felt you were really in the zone. Write down every step you took to accomplish each project, from start to finish. Think about how enjoyable each step was and rate it, on a scale from 1 to 10, with 10 being the most enjoyable. Now, focus on the steps that you rated 8 or higher. You should see a pattern that relates specifically to the kind of thinking that's occurring when you're in the zone. You could be working alone, as part of a team, or both. The type of thinking you are using to accomplish those steps is your genius in action.

If you can't think of any moments when you were in the zone, you may not be using your genius very often in your current job. This experience is not all that uncommon. It means you've probably been trying to change yourself to fit the job rather than embrace who you are. Never fear—if that is the case, you have the most opportunity for improving your current experience of work. Instead, see if you can notice when you're most engaged at home or in your personal life. Which tasks are you naturally drawn to? What is the process or thinking that most appeals to you?

For those struggling to see it, here are some additional tips for determining when you are in the zone at work:

- Slow down. Often we go through our days so quickly, we don't pay attention to the moments when we feel challenged and engaged.
- Start mapping out the moments when you're really bored or even frustrated at work. What is making you feel this way? Pay attention to the thinking or the tasks that you truly hate and try to turn them on their heads. See if your frustrations can help guide you to the problem-solving that you really enjoy. For example, a lot of "big idea" people get frustrated or bored with talking about normal day-to-day business operations.
- Create opportunities that will challenge you by putting

yourself in situations that seem a bit scary but exciting: these are the bread crumbs that will lead you to your genius. Track what you're feeling when you don't quite have the solution to a problem, but it feels like one is just around the corner. Pay attention to the moment when insight finally strikes. Where were you? What were you doing? Who were you with?

After you have tracked the moments when you're in the zone, take the data you've collected and ask yourself the following questions:

- What patterns are emerging?
- What is the thinking that I am doing that is most enjoyable?
- Is there a single type of problem that I am solving?
- How do I approach problem-solving differently from others around me?

ASK A COLLEAGUE: WHAT'S MY GENIUS?

Often, others can see your genius more clearly than you can. If you can't put a finger on what your genius might be, survey five to ten of your coworkers that know you best and have worked closely with you. Ask them:

1. What have you enjoyed most about working with me?
2. How would you describe my unique approach to my role?
3. How has working with me impacted your work experience or business results? What was the biggest change?

Once you receive feedback from your peers, compare what they say to the notes you took when you were tracking the in-the-zone moments. Do you see any patterns?

Identify Your Genius by Revisiting Your Life Story

Reviewing your past through the lens of your genius is another way to get more insight into yourself. You might find it hard to detangle your own ideas of success and potential career choices from the beliefs of your parents, mentors, and heroes. That's OK. Many of us make career decisions based on what others think, maybe more than we realize. There are hundreds of ways to rationalize taking a job that might not be the right fit: the money is good, it looks great on your resume, you are following some sort of plan that has been handed down by a well-meaning friend or family member, or you just don't know yourself well enough yet, so you choose the option that seems the most prestigious. After answering the following questions, you will be able to release the expectations you have been living up to and identify the path that is truly best for you.

The first set of questions in each part of the exercise requires short answers; the second set of questions asks you to reflect on your previous answers. Take your time with the reflections—they are meant to jog your memory, like a journal, so write as much as you can remember without overthinking your answer. Later, you'll review these questions from a different perspective, so the more details you can provide, the better.

PART 1: CHILDHOOD

What were your parents' occupations, and how have they impacted what you do for a living, if at all?

_____

_____

_____

_____

What were you known for as a kid (ages 0 to 8)? What were your interests or favorite games to play? Do any activities stand out to you as unique?

_____

_____

_____

_____

What school subjects were you good at?

_____

_____

_____

What, if any, key messages about your performance or potential did you receive from your teachers?

_____

_____

_____

_____

Reflection

Observe the previous answers as if you were reading someone else's biography. What unique activities were you drawn to as a kid and why? These may be clues to your genius.

_____

_____

_____

_____

Were you more confident about your abilities as you matured, or did you become less confident? Usually, confidence comes when your work is validated by getting good grades or getting the approval of your parents. Some children peak early with confidence and then find their confidence waning by their teen years, when schoolwork gets harder or their social life becomes more challenging.

_____

_____

_____

_____

PART 2: THE COLLEGE/EARLY ADULTHOOD YEARS

Did you go to college? If not, why, and what did you do instead?

_____

_____

_____

_____

If you went to college, how was your experience with choosing and getting accepted into a college? What were the challenging and rewarding aspects of this process?

_____

_____

_____

_____

What was your focus of study, and why did you choose this?

_____

_____

_____

_____

What were your dreams for your career after college? What about those dreams inspired you?

_____

_____

_____

_____

What feedback, if any, did you get from professors, mentors, and friends who played a role in what you did after college?

_____

_____

_____

If you didn't go to college, what were your first few jobs like, and why were you doing them? What was your vision for your adult life at this stage?

_____

_____

_____

_____

Reflection

In our college years, we often feel a lot of pressure to decide how we want to start our careers, and even how we want the rest of our lives to play out. How did you feel about the fact that you were responsible for knowing where your life would go from this point forward?

_____

_____

_____

_____

PART 3: JOBS

First Job

What was your first job? What did you do, and why did you take that job?

_____

_____

_____

_____

What tasks were you responsible for? Which did you enjoy? Which did you dislike?

_____

_____

_____

How did you feel about your ability to be successful at this stage?

_____

_____

_____

Second Job

What was your second job, and why did you take that job?

_____

_____

_____

How was this different from or similar to the first job?

_____

_____

_____

What tasks were you responsible for? Which did you enjoy? Which did you dislike?

_____

_____

What thoughts or understanding did you have about your innate strengths and weaknesses at work at this point?

_____

_____

_____

_____

List every job you have had since the first two and write down:

- What you enjoyed about each job
- What you did not enjoy about each job

Feel free to mention any specific breakthroughs or stories related to these jobs that could be relevant to feedback you received, your performance, or your self-awareness.

Job 3:

_____

_____

_____

Job 4:

_____

_____

_____

Job 5:

_____

_____

_____

Job 6:

_____

_____

_____

Job 7:

_____

_____

_____

Current Job:

_____

What sequence of events led you to what you are doing now?

_____

_____

What do you enjoy most about this job? What do you enjoy least?

_____

_____

_____

Reflection

What are the consistent themes with your past jobs and your current job that surround the tasks you most enjoy? What are the consistent ways of thinking or problem-solving that are related to the tasks you most enjoy? Answer the same questions for aspects of your job you do not enjoy.

_____

_____

_____

Were there any socially motivated reasons why you worked at any of these jobs? Was any sort of validation attached to your doing well? Did the company or group value a certain skill that you wanted to possess because people who demonstrated that skill earned the highest salaries or were valued the most?

_____

_____

_____

PART 4: FINAL ANALYSIS

What are the consistent themes from each section that reveal your genius (the kind of thinking that you most enjoy doing and that leads to your most effective work)?

_____

_____

_____

_____

1. Based on your reflections in parts 1–3, what is the way of thinking that you most often used?

    _____

    _____

    _____

2. Write a three-word description of that skill here:

    _____

    _____

    _____

3. Use a thesaurus and find a few other ways to describe it. This language will become the basis for naming your genius:

    _____

    _____

    _____

4. How do you feel about the language you used above to describe your genius? Do you see your genius as valuable? Could you explain its value and use to others?

    _____

    _____

    _____

Explain the value of your genius here:

_____

_____

_____

_____

Name Your Genius

Choosing language to describe your genius is like picking your own superhero name. I have found that creating a name for your genius is the best way to not only honor it but also remember it. It's hard to describe ourselves to others, and in the absence of specific language, we default to using general terms that could be applied to almost anyone. Words like *smart, motivated,* and *hardworking* all sound great, but what do they actually mean? When I share that my genius is an Insight Excavator and explain what that means, it feels clear, descriptive, and personal. It allows someone else to connect easily with the value that I offer.

Review the three-word description you came up with in the previous exercise. Are there stronger words you can use? Are there more accurate synonyms to describe your exact strengths? Does the language clearly define your thought process?

Now, create a phrase that best describes your genius. Practice using it. Does it feel right? Is it enjoyable to share with others? If it's not, keep playing around with the wording. You know you've hit on the right phrase when it describes you so well that you finally feel as though others can understand you.

Here are some of my favorite genius names and descriptions. Can you find your genius in any of these suggestions?

Process Creation: Making Everything Work Better

- Chaos-to-Order Problem-Solver: You thrive by bringing order to chaotic situations.

- Ideal Process Developer: You can easily create processes that bring order to disorganized situations.

- Improvement Strategist: You are constantly looking for ways to improve processes, people, and work by streamlining the way things operate.

- Needle Finder: You are driven by the process of finding solutions that are extremely hard to find.

- Process Architect: You are innately drawn to figuring out the clear steps needed to make things happen in an organized and efficient manner.

- Good-to-Great Strategist: You are challenged by taking an existing process or business function from good to great.

Visionary: Redefining the World

- Barrier-Breaking Visionary: You are challenged when you're able to think outside the box and see beyond conventional wisdom.

- Opportunity Excavator: You start with a visionary idea and begin to refine it by unearthing opportunities in creative places.

- Innovative Idea Strategist: You are challenged and engaged by tackling problems and challenges that lead to forging a new path.

- Possibility Architect: You are intellectually fired up by the act of tackling seemingly impossible problems and finding and building rare solutions.

- Vision Strategist: You bring people together to form a vision or a big movement, and then help create a clear path as to how it is manifested.

- Strategic Visionary: You're exceptional at creating a vision and outlining the steps needed to achieve that vision.

- Visionary Change Maker: You are challenged when you are making big changes that are targeted toward helping people, society, or an organization.

Strategist: Creating the Path

- Analytical Solution Strategist: You're challenged by pulling back the curtain on small and large problems and solving them by learning new concepts and analytics. You are bored by problem-solving that does not involve learning something new.

- Efficiency Strategist: You are challenged and engaged by reviewing problems from every angle and creating better, more efficient ways to reach the end result.

- People Strategist: Your innate ability is in the process of connecting with people, getting their buy-in, and being able to deliver what they need through providing the right personnel-related solutions.

- Possibility Strategist: You are challenged by thinking big and creating something beautiful from something basic; and by creating something new that has never been thought of before.
- Results Strategist: You are challenged when presented with a result to achieve and thrive in creating the process that will ensure a good result is attained consistently.
- Training Results Strategist: You are challenged and engaged by achieving a result through training others on a process or product.
- Solutions Excavator: You have a unique and powerful way of unearthing creative solutions.

Synthesizing: Bringing People and Ideas Together

- Collaboration Strategist: You're challenged and engaged by bringing people together in order to solve a problem.
- Diagnostic Problem-Solver: You ask questions to understand the entire problem or scenario, and you zero in on a clear and actionable solution.
- Discerning Ideator: You are most challenged when you are dissecting or breaking down problems and then generating

lots of creative solutions on how they can be improved upon or moved forward.

- Synthesis Expert: You are challenged by the process of bringing multiple concepts together to form one hypothesis or solution.

Catalyzing: Igniting Opportunity

- Connection Catalyst: You're challenged by approaching problems via the connections that you can create in order for things to get done.

- Holistic Crisis Problem-Solver: You are challenged by solving problems that occur in a crisis—your balanced ability to see all angles is even more appreciated and needed when times get tough.

- Social Advocate: You are challenged by thinking through decisions and always considering the people side of things. You innately think in terms of how everything will impact people.

- Team Maximizer: You're exceptional at solving team efficiency problems that don't have an obvious solution.

Builders: Ideas and Structures

- Creative Results Architect: You are totally engaged when you are able to dive into a challenge and engineer an unconventional result to solve a problem.

- Deal Conductor: You can manage multiple work streams at the same time in rapid formation, while working toward a common high-impact result.

- Design Strategist: You are challenged by devising unique ways to create design. It's in the creative process of design that you thrive.

- Experience Producer: You are engaged by the process of creating a sensory experience, such as an event (versus a tangible product).

- Innovative Rebuilder: You are challenged by the process of taking something apart and rebuilding it into something that works better.

- Language and Idea Architect: You are in the zone when you're coming up with a new idea that no one has thought of before or putting words together that make something compelling.

- New Business Growth Strategist: You are driven by thinking about growth and, more specifically, growing a business. It's exciting for you to think of a variety of business growth challenges and come up with solutions.

How Your Personality Informs Your Genius

Your personality is something you were born with. It is how you engage with the world. It evolves over the course of your life and influences your particular genius. The standard identification of personality type is the Myers-Briggs Type Indicator (MBTI). The MBTI is an introspective, self-reported questionnaire that defines how people perceive the world around them and make decisions. It is based on a theory proposed by noted psychologist Carl Jung, who believed that there are four principal psychological functions by which humans experience the world—sensation, intuition, feeling, and thinking—and that one of these four functions is dominant for each person most of the time.[14] According to Jung, we have specific preferences in the way we take part in these functions, which are critical in forming our personal interests, needs, values, and motivations.

Understanding your personality is important because it helps you make sense of how you engage with the world and your work. When you understand yourself and your motivations better, you can approach work in a manner that best suits your style, including managing time, identifying the best environments for decision-making, and dealing with stress. This self-knowledge can help you better navigate your workplace's culture and cope with change. It's even more important to understand the basic characteristics of your personality when you're working on a team because it can help you identify potential solutions to conflicts that arise. The more you know about your personality and can communicate that information to others, the more easily you can diffuse potential conflicts or make choices that best serve you and your career.

Jung's model regards psychological type as innate: people are born with a preferred way of being. The MBTI sorts these differences into four pairs of opposites, with a resulting sixteen possible psychological types. One type is not any better than the other—the benefit comes simply from knowing who you are.

Your genius is not necessarily reflected in your personality, but your personality will inform your genius. As we have discussed, your genius is the way of thinking or problem-solving that you most like to do. If part of your personality includes introversion, which means you derive energy from thinking through problems on your own, you may find that working alone is the right environment to maximize the use of your genius. An extrovert, or someone who likes to think and process by speaking with others, might have the same genius as you but feels more in the zone when she is working with a team of people. That personality difference will make the way each person uses her genius different from the other.

Your personality and your genius are two distinctive aspects of who you are, and it's important for your personal and professional selves to understand both of them. Your genius defines the kind of work you will be most successful doing, and your personality will help you find the right environment for you, including the kind of people you'll be interacting with and how the work you'll be doing will be applied.

Know Your Coworkers' Personalities

Being able to talk about your personality type helps clarify to others the lens through which you perceive the world. For instance, feelers and thinkers assess situations from two different perspectives, emotion versus rational thought. It's helpful to know the personality types of the people you're working with so you can understand their perspective as well as your own. You can use the Myers-Briggs test for determining the personality types of your colleagues, as long as they're game for taking the test and sharing their results with you (find the test online at humanmetrics.com). I find that when conflict arises at work, the underlying cause is likely the meshing of different personality types. I have worked with a variety of clients who were struggling with perception issues in their office. By simply helping them understand each of their coworkers' personalities—and their Zone of Genius—my clients were able to see that the behaviors they were taking personally were really just the way the other person was wired. With this knowledge, they were able to make better decisions on how to interact with this person in the future.

Using Your Genius at Work

Once you have identified your genius, you'll realize that you have a powerful capability within you just waiting to be exercised. Finding the connection between your genius and your personality allows you to understand the precise work you should be doing, as well as the ideal environment for you to operate in. Since I am an Insight Excavator and an extrovert, I need to be working with other people to be in the zone. I'm happiest when I'm having deep discussions with my clients to uncover patterns within their responses to my questions that allow for me to identify insights. This is a starting point for meaningful change in their lives. I wouldn't be as happy or engaged with my work if I wasn't interacting with others on a regular basis.

Understanding your genius and how you can use it will help you describe what you bring to the table during a job interview or performance review. By explaining what you're good at and what you're not good at, you are showing how you will add value to the position you're applying for. Knowing your genius is the first step toward guiding a conversation about finding or creating the right job fit for you, not you for it.

Within your current job, you can use your genius to maximize your potential, meet the challenges that you are excited about, and reframe or delegate the ones you aren't. Look at how you're prioritizing your time and the work you're managing. Most of us usually have more work than we can realistically accomplish. Find out if you can prioritize your load and delegate the tasks that don't light you up. Through that act of prioritizing and delegating, you can spend more time and effort on the work that is aligned with who you are and delegate the work that isn't. You can also get the right support to help meet those obligations.

My client Miranda's genius was as a Crisis Problem-Solver. She thrived when things went wrong, and she was known as being levelheaded even in the worst of circumstances. Miranda began to notice that she was asked to resolve lots of crises in her office and realized that instead of being frustrated or annoyed that she had to solve yet another problem, she started seeing the crisis moments as huge opportunities for her to shine. Tracking the frequency that others asked her to solve their problems also gave her the awareness that she should be spending even more of her time on crisis situations. She started rethinking the portion of her work that wasn't crisis-orientated. She started delegating run-of-the-mill tasks to other people, and she advocated for evolving her role into one that was a better fit for her genius.

Customizing Work for Lower-Level Employees

If you are in an entry-level position or are an individual contributor—meaning you don't manage a team or have a lot of freedom to organize your workload—the process of integrating your genius into your job may look different from that of someone who has more control over their time. If there is no possible way for you to create or find a project or set of tasks that is more aligned with your genius, that may be a sign that your job isn't the right one for you. However, you may have the power to change your role within the company if you are able to identify a problem and a solution, which is exactly where your genius comes in handy. Have a conversation with your manager and mention the type of work that is a better fit for you. Ask if he or she can help you find opportunities that are better suited for you. Or, show your manager how you can provide more value to the company by solving problems outside of your current role. Providing solutions to problems is a great way to demonstrate leadership. You may be surprised at how receptive others are to this kind of approach.

If you're not able to use your genius in your current role as much as you would like but see a potentially better fit within your company, it might be worth it to bide your time and stick it out at your current job until you can get promoted or switch departments. Knowing that you can't fully use your genius now, but will in the future, is a much better way to operate then feeling like you don't know why you are feeling stuck. However, there are still ways for you to maximize your experience while planning your next move. The rest of the book will cover behaviors you can start cultivating that will not only keep you more engaged but also set you up for guaranteed success once you're in a role that is the perfect fit.

How to Say No

Your manager will assume you're in the right job unless you say otherwise—after all, a manager can't read your mind. It's import-ant to initiate conversations with your manager to discuss potential opportunities to create a better fit between your genius and the work you are doing every day—sometimes even by turning down projects or assignments that clearly do not align with your genius. The more you take the lead on creating a good fit between the work you are given and your skills and expertise, the better it is for the organization and for you.

You may be concerned that saying no to a project or task could be risky—won't your manager think you're slacking off or that you're not a team player? It's possible that they might, and that's why the way you frame the conversation is incredibly important. Be sure to focus the discussion around your desire to do the best possible job at each task and your belief that the company will benefit by using your abilities to the fullest. Have the discussion in person, not over email, and bring any evidence of past successes you might have to illustrate the points you want to make about your strengths. In the end, even if your manager isn't willing to move the task off your plate, hopefully they will be impressed by the thought you're putting into your performance and will remember the conversation when other assignments come up.

If you do have the ability to decline assignments, it's important when doing so that you suggest specific work that would be a better fit for you, or reframe the assignment so that it better plays to your strengths and still allows the desired outcome. Another tactic is to find someone who wants to take on the work that isn't right for you and recommend this person as a willing alternative resource. In these situations, the work is still getting done, and it's being handled by someone who is better equipped to do it well.

If you're struggling to offload tasks that aren't a great fit for your genius, start by analyzing the work overall. Is there any way to bring more of your genius into this work? For example, you may be able to take a boring or laborious task and create a new process to make it more efficient. Are there ways you can proactively expand your role to include work that is a better fit and will help your team or organization achieve its goals? Be creative and don't be afraid to push the envelope of possibility. After all, being bold is a leadership trait, so the right company will recognize your efforts, see your high potential, and want to help you be happy, fulfilled, and effective.

What to Do If You Can't Use Your Genius at Work

If you rarely use your genius at work, it's difficult to find ways to use it more frequently, and you don't have a clear sense of when you might advance within the company to a better-fitting role, it's probably time to change jobs. This might be a scary realization, but remember that putting in the effort to find work that aligns with your genius is a great investment in your future happiness and success.

The good news is that once you have identified what your

genius is, the entire world of work is open to you. Your genius can be applied to almost any industry. This may sound counter-intuitive (i.e., *If my genius is a Design Strategist, don't I have to work in a design firm?*), but there are infinite ways you can apply your genius to your career. The key is knowing what it is and then being able to speak with authority on its value. For example, if you are a Solution Excavator, you are challenged when you are solving problems amid chaos. You can see through the data and other variables to find an easy solution. This genius can be applied to many different problems in a variety of different industries, whether it's technology, finance, or something else altogether.

Advocate for who you are and be proactive about seeking opportunities that are a better fit. Industries and jobs are changing at such a rapid rate that job-specific knowledge is becoming less important. The problems we face at work are always changing, but the need for people who solve problems is only increasing. You just need to be able to speak about the ways you best like to problem-solve. If you have spent years working in real estate, but you have a strong desire to shift to the health industry, show how you solved problems in real estate and apply that genius to the health industry or to a specific role you're interested in.

A lot of people are waiting around for the perfect job to land in their lap versus going out and uncovering one or even creating one, either as an entrepreneur or in an organization that will allow them to capitalize on their strengths. Taking initiative, showing how you can fill a need, and being proactive about seeking opportunities will put you far ahead of the majority of other job-seekers.

Ben Knew His Genius

Most people would say that Ben had a perfect life. He grew up in a comfortable home, had a secure childhood, and got an Ivy League education. When he graduated he spent a short time in the corporate world before he and two colleagues decided to start their own company. Ben became the CEO, and the other two were his cofounders. Within a few years the company grew, and by the time Ben came to me, he had three hundred employees. Even though on paper it looked like Ben was successful, he couldn't help feeling that something was missing—like he'd just been checking boxes his whole life. And his disengagement was starting to affect the company's results.

Ben reached out to me because he had received the negative yet constructive feedback that he wasn't holding his executive team accountable. Ben told me that he perceived himself as a big-picture thinker, a dreamer, a deal maker. Getting bogged down in the day-to-day minutiae of running a company was his worst nightmare. Consequently, all too often he'd let little tasks fall through the cracks. However, these small tasks had a way of snowballing into big problems—and not only were his employees expressing frustration over lack of clarity about their mandates, but the board of directors also was noticing.

There seemed to be no way to get around the fact that Ben was failing to meet his responsibilities, and he had begun to dream of escape. "I just want to live in the country with twenty dogs," he told me during one of our sessions. Were Ben's dreams about such a drastic lifestyle shift grounded in a true longing for life in the country, or was he just experiencing fatigue because of a poor work fit?

When we started working together, Ben told me about the trajectory of his life and how he found it all very predictable. What really got him excited was having big ideas that could change the world. This sounded much different from moving up to the country to live with dogs, so I knew that suggestion wasn't what he was really after.

We worked through the genius exercises, and he talked to me about how he felt when he was in the zone. I could see that Ben was creative and strategic, and he liked to bring others along in his thinking. He felt energized when his ideas evolved as a result of talking them through with others. He wasn't the most detail-oriented, *How can we get this done?* thinker, but he was definitely a very big *What can we do?* thinker. His warmth and genuine style inspired others. It was obvious to both of us that he wanted to be out in the world making deals. We called his genius a Possibility Architect because he felt most inspired by learning something new and then taking that information and creating a new big idea.

Once we identified Ben's genius, it was obvious we had to figure out a way for him to use it more often in the office. He had two cofounders, so we devised a way to break up the work Ben found tedious and give it to one of the partners who was better suited for those tasks. That left him more time to do what he really loved, which was to focus on new possibilities, new clients, even a potential sale of the business. His personality type also was helpful in providing direction on specific solutions. He was an extrovert who preferred structure, but he was also comfortable with a little bit of chaos. Ben loved speaking in front of groups, specifically answering unplanned questions. His comfort level with people and an unpredictable scenario meant that a casual question-and-answer structure was ideal for him and was a setting where his Possibility Architect genius emerged. He could paint a vision for his team and inspire them with possibilities. Often, new possibilities would come from the back-and-forth banter.

I suggested that he hire a chief of staff—a detail-oriented, project-planning person who would report directly to Ben. He had never considered hiring this kind of employee, and I explained that a lot of senior executives and CEOs have this type of operational assistance. Ben immediately thought of Beth, a junior worker in his organization who would be perfect for that role. It was important for him to know that, as an extrovert, he could talk through ideas with Beth, using her as a sounding board for his thoughts.

A few weeks later, Ben came back to see me. Based on his Performance Tracker data, it was clear that his boredom and frustration were waning. His scores for both the Challenge and the Impact sections were rising week over week. He was regularly experiencing three or more weekly moments of being in the zone, up from zero. He was also scoring himself a 4 for his Impact section, which meant he noticed that the impact he was having was the one he wanted 80 percent of the time. The work we had done together to identify his genius allowed him to focus on the tasks he enjoyed while delegating the tasks he had been struggling with.

He had hired Beth as his chief of staff, and she was acting as his operational right-hand person. Her job was to make sure everyone on the executive team was supported in their operational duties. Ben could show up to the meetings and run them, and she would be there to provide all the details and ensure that everyone at the table was being held accountable for their deliverables. This one hire was a game changer because it freed Ben from feeling like he had to do all the mundane CEO tasks he hated. And as a Possibility Architect, he could spend his time making deals and starting new initiatives. Ben is now more content with his role because he knows how to deliver consistently, even on the parts of his job that aren't as exciting to him, while also spending most of his time doing the work that really fires him up. Compared to the feeling of being stuck and unclear when we first met, he feels energized by the deeper self-knowledge and awareness that he can now bring to his job every day.

The Next Step: Moving into the Zone of Genius

Once you understand your genius, you can start to develop the Genius Habit at work. This means seeing new ways to use your genius, being more productive, and ultimately having more fun at work—eventually with little to no concentrated effort. By knowing who you are and what you do best, you can choose the activities that make you feel more fulfilled and excited about your job. The next step is to create a Zone of Genius—a space where you are combining your unique skills with your ultimate purpose.

PART II

IMPACT

CHAPTER 4

QUIT FOLLOWING YOUR PASSION AND FIND YOUR PURPOSE

Question: When was the last time you felt really fulfilled at work?

Genius Action Plan: Identify Your Core Emotional Challenge—and Use It to Find Your Purpose

Are you as sick as I am of hearing about how important it is to "follow your passion?" Unfortunately, this well-meaning advice to find work we're passionate about has sent too many people on a frustrating quest to turn a hobby into a career. The problem with following passions is that they are, by definition, fleeting—they burn hard but die fast. Your passions are what bring you joy in the moment. They don't define who you are or what you are good at. And they certainly have very little to do with your genius.

I've met hundreds of people who followed their passions into the workforce. Some of them really enjoyed a single class in college and thought that would point them in a particular direction. Others like food and think about working in the restaurant business, and some think their love of fitness means they should become a personal trainer. For many, following a passion might seem like an obvious quick fix to career dissatisfaction, but it often doesn't address the real problem: without focusing on their genius, these people really don't know what kind of work is right for them. They don't know what value they bring to the table or how they like to work. These same people end up being disappointed and even depressed when they find that the work related to their passion is not right for them. As a result, they may be turned off from their hobby and certainly are no better off professionally than when they started. Then, without gaining any awareness about why they are dissatisfied, they jump to the next job, following yet another passion, and are equally miserable.

Well-intentioned friends and family may dole out career advice based on their observances of your passions and interests. For instance, I have a passion for cooking. I enjoy it because I don't do it that often, and what I love about it is not so much the actual meal planning or creation—it's bringing people together over a meal and the challenge of testing my culinary limits. Plenty of people have come to my dinner parties and said, "Oh my gosh, everything is so delicious! You should open a restaurant."

If I had less awareness of my genius and purpose, I'd seriously consider it, possibly thinking, *Maybe they're right: I should ditch the hard work of running my own business and go to work for someone else as a chef.* But because I know my genius is as an Insight Excavator, where I can see patterns in data, draw insights from those patterns, and turn the insights into action, I would only change careers if the opportunity offered me a way to use my genius every day and was in line with my career vision. As a chef, I would not have the opportunity to engage in the kind of work that really gets me fired up—unless I spent the majority of my time speaking to diners about their experiences eating in the restaurant, looking for patterns in their responses, and deciding how to change the ordering of the ingredients to better match what the customers liked most! But that's not how the majority of chefs spend their time. In fact, I would be better suited to the position of restaurant manager. But when other people suggest I run a restaurant, they aren't thinking through the reality of the day-to-day or how the actual job of a chef would be the wrong fit.

Some lucky people may be able use their passion to lead them to a career path that uses their genius and provides them with fulfillment. A passion can provide direction, but if you can't connect it to your genius, ultimately it won't be enough to find the job that brings you sustainable challenge. For instance, I love fitness: I work out five days a week. Maybe I would have been successful working for a company like Fitbit or an apparel giant like Nike or Under Armour. But if I had decided to follow my passion for fitness directly to a company within that industry, without applying my knowledge of my genius, I could have ended up in a part of the business that didn't match my skill set, such as certain areas of sales or marketing. In that case, I may have ended up bored and frustrated in a job that I felt *should* be perfect for me—but wasn't.

As wonderful as it might sound to find a job you enjoy within an area you're passionate about, I have found that the best fit is a job that involves the method of work you're exceptional at—your genius—combined with another aspect of your life that is perhaps even more meaningful and longer-lasting than your passions—your *purpose*. Your purpose is the impact you make on others that provides meaning to your life. The difference between passion and purpose is the key. Passions are great in the short run, but your purpose is more lasting and will ultimately bring you deeper fulfillment.

Your purpose is influenced by your personal history and your core emotional challenge: it is a positive expression of a negative experience (or experiences) that has impacted you at the deepest level. Your core emotional challenge represents a recurring emotional reaction to a variety of events in your life or one major event that changed the course of your life from that point forward. As a result of the profound effect this had on you, you find that helping someone else navigate this same challenge is extremely meaningful. If you can use what you've learned—even on a subconscious level—to help others, you've found your purpose. And because of this connection between your own past hurts and resolving them, your purpose is deeper than getting a job in the restaurant industry because you're passionate about food or becoming a talent booker because you love music.

Ideally, your purpose will endure and provide endless motivation for you by having an impact on others that is directly linked to it, because your core emotional challenge will always be part of who you are. If you are having an impact on something greater than yourself, whether it's another person, the planet, or any other cause, and it is directly connected to your own personal experiences, you will easily find work enjoyable even when it is challenging. But when that personal connection is missing, even nonprofit work for the most compelling cause can feel like an obligation, rather than pure joy.

The Purpose of Purpose

Many of us started our careers by trying to answer a seemingly simple question: What do you want to be when you grow up? Some of us would answer with our hearts on our sleeves: astronauts, police officers, even the president of the United States. Some of us picked the opposite of our parents' experience: what they did seemed cool enough, but it wasn't for us. Or we saw their dissatisfaction with their careers and made a decision to forge a different path. Maybe we had already started to feel like certain aspirations were out of our grasp, so we started to manage our own expectations.

This question pops up in other forms, like "What are you going to major in?" "What's your plan after college?" and "What kind of job are you going to get?" What all these questions have in common is their focus on the future—the implication is that at some point we will become something bigger or better than what we currently are. They also focus on the *what*: the job we will do, the industry we will work in, the title we will aspire to have.

I'd argue that we're asking the wrong questions from day one, and it leads a lot of people down the wrong path. With an unending variety of industries, career paths, and technology that allows us to do almost anything from anywhere, it's shocking to me that, according to Gallup in 2017, 68 percent of Americans are not engaged with their work. In order to truly find engagement and satisfaction at work, we should stop focusing so much on the *what* and think more about the *why*.[15]

Luckily, there is a way to course-correct. Discovering your purpose is how you can recognize the specific impact that fulfills you, by understanding *why* you are drawn to it. In fact, knowing the kind of impact that motivates you is a career must. Without it, you are missing an essential ingredient for success.

Adam Grant, a professor at the Wharton School of Business, has researched the connection between personal fulfillment and impact at work and examined what motivates workers in settings that range from call centers and mail-order pharmacies to swimming pool lifeguard squads. In each of these situations, Grant has found that employees who know why their work has a meaningful, positive impact on others are not just happier than those who don't; they are vastly more productive.[16]

In one research experiment published in 2007, Grant surveyed employees at a public university's call center who were asked to phone potential contributors and ask for donations. In this study, Grant and a team of researchers arranged for a group of call center workers to meet with scholarship students who were recipients of the school's fund-raising largesse. It wasn't a long meeting, just a five-minute session where the workers were able to interact with the students who benefited from donations to the university. Over the next month, that little chat made a big difference. The callers who had interacted with the scholarship students spent more than twice as many minutes on the phone with potential donors as callers who hadn't attended the meeting and brought in vastly more money: a weekly average of $503.22, up from $185.94. This research demonstrates clearly that knowing the impact of your work affects your motivation and performance.

A second theory on motivation comes from Daniel Pink. In his book *Drive*, Pink writes that there's a gap between what science knows and what business does. Science tells us clearly that rewards such as money and benefits don't motivate employees; however, businesses disregard the research and continue to use these kinds of rewards in hopes of boosting performance and pro-ductivity. Often, those benefits do lure high-quality employees into particular jobs. However, free food, game rooms, and even raises do nothing for the day-to-day motivation needed to enjoy work. This paradox leaves employees feeling confused: why don't they feel more motivated in the midst of receiving so many perks? But there really is no mystery: perks are nice to have, but they don't help you feel more challenged in your job, nor do they pro-vide the long-lasting fulfillment that satisfying work does.

Pink found that the real drivers of motivation are:

1. Autonomy—the desire to direct our own lives.
2. Mastery—the urge to get better at something that matters to you (which I believe is linked to genius).
3. Purpose—the yearning to participate in the service of some-thing larger than ourselves.

Pink writes:

The first two legs of the tripod, autonomy and mastery, are essential. But for proper balance we need a third leg—purpose, which provides a context for its two mates. Autonomous people working toward mastery perform at very high levels. But those who do so in the service of some greater objective can achieve even more. The most deeply motivated people—not to mention those who are most productive and satisfied—hitch their desires to a cause larger than themselves.

Purpose is clearly essential for being motivated at work. It seems simple enough; if you understand how your job changes people's lives in a way that is meaningful to you, you are more likely to end up having endless energy for your work.

Being happy at work is linked to understanding your genius and having the right level of challenge—the intellectual fulfillment of the daily tasks. Finding your work meaningful, on the other hand, is connected to your impact at work tapping into your purpose. There's nothing more gratifying than knowing that your work is making the world a better place.

FIND A COMPANY WITH PURPOSE

In today's world, a clear purpose can be one of a business's biggest assets. Purpose-driven companies such as TOMS, Patagonia, and Warby Parker have built engagement and consumer loyalty among people who share their values. Customers are more likely to buy products from a company that aligns with their purpose, and these companies are often able to attract great talent by putting a stake in the ground for what they stand for.

Genius Action Plan: Identify Your Core Emotional Challenge—and Use It to Find Your Purpose

Your core emotional challenge is a formative part of your identity that you may not be conscious of. I discovered the power of the core emotional challenge through my fervent quest to uncover what motivates and excites me about work. Once I understood it, I saw that it was the answer to finding my purpose.

I grew up on a dairy farm near Charlottesville, Virginia, and I always felt different from the rest of my family. I felt like I wasn't in the right place and that my parents and siblings didn't get who I really was. The most obvious difference was that I'm an extrovert, and the rest of my family is mostly introverted. At school I was teased for being a farm girl and for participating in community theatre, which was something I loved to do and made me feel alive. I knew that I ultimately wanted a life very different from what I experienced during my childhood. I wanted to live in a big city. I wanted to see the world. Yet my family couldn't relate to my dreams and aspirations. I remember telling my dad that I was going to be living in a city, working as an executive, and he laughed and said, "OK, Laura, let's see." His reaction to my dreams always communicated disbelief in my ability to do things differently than how everyone around me was doing them.

It wasn't obvious to me how I was going to attain the life I envisioned for myself, but I knew if I wanted it, I would have to be the one to make it happen. Even though I was nurtured and loved by my parents, they didn't know how to help me think about my future in the way I craved. The message I got from my family was the one-size-fits-all approach to life: go to school, go to college, get a job. When I was interested in pursuing something slightly different, like studying in Sweden for a year in college, my parents chuckled. They thought it was another one of my crazy ideas and asked questions like, "Oh, Laura, how are you going to do that? And more importantly, how are you going to pay for it?" Despite their questioning on the front end, I applied and got accepted to a study abroad program, and they supported my decision to go.

When I returned home from Sweden I was happier than I had ever been, feeling like an entirely different person after my life-changing experience. But how could I explain it to my family? How could I sum up everything I'd learned in that year? While I was away we only spoke on the phone a few times and exchanged a handful of letters. They couldn't possibly notice the changes I was feeling in my own transformation into a young woman. I had gained a new sense of confidence and the feeling that I could thrive anywhere. I felt that my life had fundamentally changed, that I could achieve anything I wanted. Surely, my family would see that now too. As my father and I drove to a restaurant a few days after I had returned from Sweden, I took out my photographs, each showing a different part of my journey. In one, I was on a boat going from Sweden to Finland for a weekend. In another, I was hosting a party at my apartment. In yet another I was on a week-long trip to England with a friend, eating bread we had baked to save money for the trip.

"It seems like you just had a big party and my money was wasted," my dad said.

I felt deflated. I started crying and got out of the car. My father could never understand how and why this experience was transformative for me—how it was one of my first chances to break free from a world that felt too small, and nothing I could tell him could convince him otherwise. My heart ached.

Years later, in the early days of building my business, I spent a lot of time tracking my behavior and thinking, *What is my purpose? What is fulfilling to me?* Nothing I came up with seemed to click until one afternoon when I stepped onto a treadmill at the gym. I looked up to the row of TVs, searching for the one that *Oprah* was on, as I always did.

The guest that day described an experience that hit me hard. She shared that she felt as if nobody understood her, that she was different and struggled to fit in in a variety of environments. As the guest shared her experience, so many instances of my life where I had felt different came back to me. I realized that this woman was going through the experience of not being seen by important people in her life, and that I had often felt the same way. Tears rolled down my cheeks. For the first time, I was able to recognize and articulate a profound loss that I had experienced.

I finally understood that not being seen was a core emotional challenge for me. More than that, I could see how that feeling of not being seen had driven so much of my discontent over the years. Interestingly, in the early part of my career, I sought out jobs where I was not being seen, yet they felt comfortable to me. I accepted jobs that weren't aligned with who I was, and as a result what was expected of me to succeed was misaligned with my authentic self. My managers saw me through the lens of the job I was performing in, but they couldn't see the real me. Through working with my clients, I have seen that people often unconsciously re-create environments that mirror their family dynamics and values because they feel comfortable. That's the experience I had unconsciously been seeking at Google: a company that looked great on paper and was inside the box enough to make my parents happy. I realized how that feeling of not being seen and being misplaced and not quite right was an environment that I was recreating over and over again. These companies didn't see me for who I was or had the potential to be because I didn't see it in myself.

As I continued to seek my purpose, I thought about the most pivotal experiences in my life, such as going to Sweden, moving to South Africa for an entrepreneurial job at Capital One, and moving to New York City and starting my own business. They all involved moments when I was forced to defend what I was capable of, despite doubts from others. They were also my greatest triumphs—the times when I succeeded against the odds. Each of these decisions was considered outside the box or too risky by my family, which made me feel as if they didn't see me for who I really was. Didn't they believe that I could do everything I was trying to accomplish? They didn't understand what I was doing, and they were afraid I would fail. However, I didn't recognize their fear, which was based out of concern and love for me; I only saw that they didn't recognize in me the person I desperately wanted to be.

Once I recognized my core emotional challenge, I knew that helping others be seen for who they were was my purpose in life. And, in fact, I was already doing it! I'm always trying to make people feel seen. I do that by asking lots of questions; I'm endlessly curious about people and what motivates them. At parties I always find myself in deep conversations with other guests, talking about what they do and how they feel about their work. I can quickly see the value of who they are and try to point this out to them. I'm also drawn to movies, books, and television shows where the characters are coming into their own, usually by tapping into their strengths and believing in themselves.

Helping other people in this way was the key I had been missing in the corporate world. Once I understood my purpose and started to incorporate this practice into my business, I finally created the work that energized me. Helping clients uncover their genius and their purpose is the best way I've found to help them see themselves for the value they possess. My clients have reported time after time that knowing these two parts of themselves better is what lets them do their work more efficiently and get better results.

Most people don't know what their purpose is because they haven't taken the time to uncover their core emotional challenge, so it's no wonder that they are clueless about the impact they're having on other people, especially their colleagues. My client Robin is constantly telling her office mates what a great job they are doing. She goes above and beyond in acknowledging their contributions to the team. She has been doing this her entire work life, long before we met. But she never realized or thought about the impact her encouraging words made on others until we talked about it. When I pointed out to her that her desire to acknowledge others was connected to her core emotional challenge, she had an aha moment. Robin never realized that her supportive behavior was exactly what she had wanted from her mother, but never received. What's more, she was supporting her colleagues all the time without even realizing it. Filling out the Performance Tracker helped her pinpoint how great acknowledging others made her feel, and how motivating that good feeling was for her at work. By identifying this purpose, she was able to do more of it, and use that purpose as an asset. What's more, she was able to begin to do the internal work to acknowledge herself, which allowed her to feel more confident and able to advocate for herself and the promotion she deserved.

This book is a further extension of my purpose: my hope is that once you adopt the Genius Habit, your efforts at work will be noticed, and you will be seen for who you really are.

Identify Your Core Emotional Challenge

While we've all faced and conquered a variety of challenges and obstacles, I have found that there is almost always one significant recurring challenge or theme that comes up in my clients' lives. The following exercise is meant to uncover your core emotional challenge by looking at patterns from your past. Be prepared to do some digging and deep thinking. Be honest with your answers and don't worry how it all translates to your purpose. Once you've completed the questions, you will go back and review them to see where ideas about your purpose may emerge.

PART 1: CHILDHOOD AGES 5 TO 18

What was the best part of your childhood from ages 5 to 18? What was the most challenging part? Why?

_____

_____

_____

_____

What was the best part of your high school days? What was the most challenging part? Why?

_____

_____

_____

_____

_____

Were you popular? Did you have good friendships? How did these friendships affect your confidence or sense of self-worth?

_____

_____

_____

_____

How would you describe your home life and your parents' relationship? Was your home life stable?

_____

_____

_____

What was the specific impact of your family on you?

_____

_____

_____

_____

How did your parents relate to you during this time in your life? Did they support your strengths? Did they have a preconceived idea of what you should do for a career or how you should live your life?

_____

_____

_____

_____

Reflection

Analyze your answers as if you were reading someone else's biography. Write down the most obvious emotional challenges from this time period:

_____

_____

_____

_____

_____

Are you currently facing any of the challenges you listed above?

_____

_____

_____

_____

PART 2: COLLEGE

If you didn't go to college, apply these questions to whatever you did for the four years following high school.

Were there any career-defining moments during this time? Meaning, did you have a significant insight or make a big decision that had a massive effect on your choice of your first job or career aspirations?

_____

_____

_____

_____

What were some of the emotional challenges you experienced during these years?

_____

_____

_____

_____

Reflection

Looking back at all the questions from this exercise, identify the core emotional challenge throughout your life that seems to have been the most significant to you. Look for the one challenge that was consistently present throughout.

_____

_____

_____

_____

Once you've figured out your core emotional challenge, or even if you still haven't, review when you are most fulfilled at work. List the moments in the past month when you have felt fulfilled by the impact you were having. Write down the specific impact you were having on other people through your work.

_____

_____

_____

_____

Resolving Your Core Emotional Challenge

Once I recognized my core emotional challenge, I realized that to be truly successful, I needed to address my own negative behavior that occurred when I wasn't feeling seen. This meant being more aware of when it happened and addressing the angst it caused within me. I don't think it's ever possible to completely erase a core emotional challenge from your life, but having a greater awareness of it can be the first step to healing.

I had to work through the emotional baggage I was carrying so that it didn't have a hold on my joy. I did a lot of rewiring of my negative mental messaging and dedicated time to the habit of having deep respect and love for myself. I was able to internalize the knowledge that my desires and goals were valid pursuits. Working on appreciating myself gave me permission to follow my dream of starting my own business and the confidence to pursue my desires and to expect to fulfill them. In essence, I learned to see myself, and I liked what I saw.

As a result of the time and thought I put into addressing my core emotional challenge, when I feel like I'm not being seen, I am better able to manage my emotions so that I no longer become derailed by them. Don't get me wrong; it still hurts when I feel that I am not seen, and I get upset and agitated when it happens. However, understanding where those emotions are coming from allows me to move through that reaction faster and get to a more productive mental space.

The process of working through many different core emotional challenges can vary. However, the work always begins by identifying your core emotional challenge and then giving to yourself what that core emotional challenge has taken away. My client Randy's core emotional challenge, for example, was not being prioritized. Whenever he felt that others' needs or priorities were unfairly being prioritized over his own, he got very upset—sometimes to the point of being unprofessional. Randy was getting constructive feedback from his manager that he wasn't a team player. However, he still received high marks for being a great manager himself because he often made his team feel like they were valued and essential. His purpose was helping people feel prioritized, but without healing this wound in himself, he had moments of coming across as off-putting to others, which was not his intention.

I asked Randy to use the Performance Tracker to document instances when he was not being prioritized. He became more conscious of how often and in what situations this tended to occur, and he built an awareness that this reaction was coming from his past and was not always relevant in the present. Then we began to rewire the negative messaging in his head that perpetuated the fear that he was not a priority to those around him. Over the course of a few months, Randy started feeling more resilient in the face of his core emotional challenge, which led to increased confidence as he began to heal his deeply engrained wound.

Today, a large part of my business is helping my clients identify their core emotional challenges and figuring out how to resolve them. I typically see two different scenarios.

The first common scenario I see is in people like Randy who have ignored the resolution of their core emotional challenge and focused only on helping others. This means he was prioritizing others with his management style, but he was completely derailed when others didn't prioritize him, which really means he wasn't doing the work to ensure that he was making himself a priority. While they can get fulfillment from helping others, these individuals can get stuck in a loop of low self-esteem and continue to struggle with negative self-talk, which coupled can be a breeding ground for low confidence, the ultimate career killer. If you never do the work to address your own issues, you may continually experience internal turmoil, anger, anxiety, or fear.

The second scenario I tend to see in my work is people who are aware of their core emotional challenge, have already begun the work of addressing it (whether consciously or subconsciously), are using it to help others, yet are not attaching this knowledge to the concept of purpose. My client Susan is an executive in a medium-size company. She is high-functioning yet lacks confidence. While she couldn't have told you exactly what her purpose was when we started working together, once we identified it, Susan suddenly felt all the pieces of her personal challenges and the way she interacted with other people come together and make sense. Susan's purpose was helping others exceed expectations by giving them a lot of support. She realized that she was already leveraging her purpose at work because she was a skilled manager, she loved her team and gave them a lot of support, and she got a lot of fulfillment out of seeing them exceed her expectations. She did have more work to do in terms of overcoming her core emotional challenge, which was exceeding expectations without support, but she could clearly see how she had been subconsciously using her own pain to fuel her interactions with others, and she was happy to take a more deliberate approach to addressing her core emotional challenge and building her confidence.

Once you identify your core emotional challenge, you may be amazed by how often you notice it surfacing through uncomfortable moments in your work and life. These are the times when you may say to yourself, *Wow, I have no idea why I am in tears over the fact that my friend just canceled our plans last minute.* While the canceled event may have been meaningless, the fact that you feel ignored could be your core emotional challenge, and a small, seemingly benign event in the present can trigger deep-seated pain from the past. Recognizing my core emotional challenge was liberating: when small events occur and cause me to feel unseen, I can step back and say to myself, *Oh wait, this is a core emotional wound. This is bringing me back to a painful event from my past. My reaction right now is a more extreme reaction than what this situation calls for.*

As you begin to notice when your triggers occur, you can begin to modify your reaction to them. According to psychologist John

Cacioppo, PhD, our brains are wired to pick up more negative information than positive.[17] In fact, our brains take in two-thirds negative and one-third positive information. This is why our general state of awareness is highly critical. However, we can compensate for this tendency by adding more positive data to any situation.

I have found that creating positive self-talk that addresses the negative chatter in our minds when we are triggered by a core emotional challenge can be a highly effective way to move forward and heal. For example, if my negative message is *I'm not being seen*, when I flip the narrative and tell myself that I'm in fact being seen, it actually calms me down. Sometimes, I just need to say, *I see myself. I'm valuable.*

Try Behavioral Modifications

You can work to reduce the power that your core emotional challenge has over you by rewiring your brain and replacing negative thought patterns with positive ones. Here are some behavioral modifications you can try.

Rewire Negative Mental Chatter

In order to rewire negative mental chatter, you first have to notice the specific messages that are manifesting in your mind. Once you do this, you can create new, more positive messages to replace the negative ones. By doing so, you literally create new neuronal pathways in your brain that connect to the thoughts of the present, instead of memories from the past. For example, if your negative chatter is telling you how unsuccessful and stupid you are, reverse this message to, *I am a smart person with a genius that is highly valuable, and as a result I will be very successful.*

As you repeat this positive statement, you should experience two benefits. The first is that you immediately feel better; the second is that you will feel more confident over time. You will see evidence that this new statement is true because you'll be more inclined to notice the aspects of your life that match the positive messages you're creating. What we think becomes a reality, which is why when you are overcome by your negative chatter, life can seem grim.

Consider Tapping

Tapping is a behavior modification therapy for shifting your neurological energy, and a mindfulness practice with a physical component that turns negative thoughts into positive affirmations. According to Jim Curtis, author of *The Stimulati Experience*, tapping is also referred to by therapists as Emotional Freedom Techniques (EFT) and combines the best practices of ancient Chinese acupressure and modern psychology. Tapping is meant to interrupt and redirect established patterns and habits. It can help you get to the root of deep emotional wounds, then help you balance the mind and body in order to change bad behaviors or feelings into ones that are more positive.

The body, like everything in the universe, is composed of energy. Lightly tapping on the meridian end points—the energy channels that connect to the organs and other systems of the body—sends a calming response. These meridian points are located primarily on the face: the eyebrow, side of the eye, under the eye, under the nose, and chin.[18] The basic technique requires you to focus on your core emotional challenge while using your fingertips to tap five to seven times each on twelve of the body's meridian points. According to Curtis, you should end the session with a positive affirmation. I suggest creating a statement that clearly defines your challenge as part of the affirmation. Someone who struggles with being understood as their core emotional challenge might say, "I understand who I am despite being different from others." By turning the expression of your challenge into a positive statement and combining that positive language with physical tapping, you can quickly reprogram your brain to turn the negative struggle into a neutral experience. Over time, you will respond less strongly to triggers as your brain stops associating the stressful situation with overwhelmingly negative emotions and responses.

Erica Reimagines Her Career

Erica is twenty-five and has been out of college for a few years. She has already pursued the jobs she thought she wanted, and she hated them. She landed what she thought should have been her dream job in the film industry but found that her entry-level position was filled with meaningless tasks. On top of that, she was not being treated particularly well. The culture of the company was less than ideal: people were always talking about each other behind their backs, colleagues weren't supportive, and politics was the currency used to get promotions. As a result, Erica was deflated from the experience and didn't feel like playing the game to rise to the top. Was this the way work was supposed to be?

Erica told me she wanted to explore her options and figure out if there was a way to find work that lit her up, wasn't exhausting, and had a positive impact on others. Together, we identified her genius as an Opportunity Designer, because Erica was all about seeing and creating opportunity. Finding new opportunities was what she liked best about the film business: she enjoyed her job when she found a script that had potential for success and played a role in making the deal happen.

Her purpose was helping others fulfill their dreams, which stemmed from her core emotional challenge of not feeling supported in her future plans. Her parents thought the idea of moving to New York and pursuing a career in film was silly; it wasn't a "real" career. She was also not encouraged or supported in her pursuit to learn the ropes of her local theater or in her interest in watching movies and eventually making films with her friends in high school. As a result, she had to fight harder to make her dreams a reality and had an ingrained sense of never feeling supported. For this reason, she loved understanding other people's dreams and helping them see how they could pursue them.

Once we identified her genius and her purpose, I helped Erica see a wider variety of jobs that she could pursue. I also helped her understand that while the job that she had been in wasn't the right fit, it didn't mean that she couldn't find a film industry job that was perfect for her. While a career in film was Erica's true passion, it was important that she find a job in which her passion was aligned with her Zone of Genius. This way, if her passion for film ever wanes, she's still going to love what she's doing as long as she's using her genius and making an impact that resonates with her purpose.

As part of our process, we explored jobs Erica never knew existed, such as being part of a film crew that worked on big sales events, or crews that helped create short films that were sold to other companies. Keeping her genius and purpose in mind, we were able to narrow down a few positions that were still entry-level but would give her more autonomy to create opportunities and allow her to have the impact that was aligned with her purpose. For each position, we dissected the actual work that she would be doing to see if there was an aspect of the job that would allow her to create opportunities. And we looked at the impact of each position and company to see if it would allow Erica to help others fulfill their dreams. Once we had a preliminary list of jobs that filled both criteria, we looked closely at the job descriptions to identify how Erica could link her genius and purpose to the specific role each company was looking to fill. I wanted her to be able to demonstrate how she saw herself adding value to the team and organization.

The company she ended up working for made training videos for various industries, and Erica worked on a team that directed and filmed fun ways to teach people key skills. She was ecstatic because she could use both her genius and her purpose, and she loved the product she was working on. She felt as if she was helping people pursue their dreams by helping them learn the particular skills they needed to succeed.

I speak with Erica often, and she tells me that while her career is just getting started, she feels like she's off to a great start. She's already charting her path to a promotion in her current company and is setting her sights on one day owning her own film agency, where she will be able to help writers and actors get their art out into the world. I have no doubt that she will do just that.

Still Not Sure What Your Purpose Is?

If you're having trouble nailing down what your purpose might be, here are some examples that might inspire you. The following purpose statements are linked to some common core emotional challenges. Reviewing these expressions of core emotional challenges may help you see your own.

Positive: being a force of positivity. If you were raised in an environment that was often critical and negative, you are fulfilled by bringing positivity to as many situations as possible.

Ideal environments: creating an environment that allows people to thrive. This purpose is rooted in a core challenge of being raised in an environment, especially at school or at home, that felt like the wrong fit. As a result, you love creating ideal environments for others to thrive in.

Opportunities: creating opportunities. If your core emotional challenge was growing up with a lack of opportunities (financial or otherwise), creating opportunities for others offers great fulfillment.

Potential: ensuring life is operating smoothly and to its highest potential. You might identify with this purpose if you were raised in a chaotic environment that did not allow you to cultivate your potential. Now, you are constantly managing situations in order to keep things running smoothly. The net result is that you are helping others operate at their full potential.

Support: exceeding expectations by supporting others. You love supporting other people and helping them to achieve great things. You may be counteracting a childhood experience during which the bar for achievement was high and support wasn't provided for you to reach that bar.

Be bold: helping others be themselves. This core emotional challenge comes from a pattern of hiding yourself because of fear of rejection. You want to help others be bold in a way that feels right for them.

Free: helping others feel free. This core emotional challenge comes from being or feeling restricted in an unhealthy way. As a result, it's fulfilling to you to help someone else feel free, unencumbered, and able to thrive as they wish.

Control: helping others feel in control. If you felt inadequate and out of control in your early years due to an unstable home life or other events, it is likely that helping others feel in control and powerful is particularly meaningful to you.

Understood: helping others feel understood despite being different. Helping others feel understood is meaningful for you because being understood by your family and close friends remains a constant challenge.

Heard: helping others find their voice. This purpose might stem from the challenge of growing up in a family where there was little to no communication or a feeling that you weren't heard. Helping others be open, find their voice, or fine-tune a message they need to share is endlessly fulfilling to you.

Different: helping others follow a different path, rather than the expected path. If you have always been drawn to a different path but were discouraged from pursuing it, helping others take the road less traveled will be exhilarating.

Failure: helping others overcome failure. This purpose comes from the core emotional challenge of dealing with the failings of others, most likely your parents or significant others. As a result, you have learned to make good decisions and avoid failures that negatively affect others. In addition, you are fulfilled by helping others with this same challenge.

Potential: helping others step outside of their comfort zone and realize their potential. You enjoy helping others step into possibility, and any activity that allows you to create that feeling for another person is rewarding. This is because you may have felt trapped, did not believe in yourself, or witnessed a parent not actualize his or her potential.

Belong: helping people find a role in which they belong. You are fulfilled by helping people find the exact role in their workplace or life in which they will shine. You are fulfilled by this because your core emotional challenge has been about feeling as though you are not often in a place where you belong and trying to identify your own place in the world.

Acceptance: making others feel accepted. You are fulfilled by being nonjudgmental and receptive to others because it's connected to a core emotional challenge of feeling like you were not accepted by your family for being who you are.

Included: making others feel included. You enjoy

helping others feel included. The reason for this is that your core emotional challenge was feeling left out, especially if you were a shy child and experienced times of feeling isolated.

Valued: making others feeling valued. If you were raised in a family where who you are was not valued, you may have been encouraged to be someone that you weren't. You therefore are fulfilled by helping others feel valued for being who they are.

Calm: helping others navigate chaos. If you had to navigate ongoing chaos throughout your childhood, you likely learned a unique skill of adaptation and being calm in the face of a storm. You are fulfilled by helping others navigate a hectic, fast-paced, or even disorganized workplace by being a voice of calm and reason.

Fairness: promoting fairness. A core emotional challenge growing up was that you felt unfairly disadvantaged or you did not get the same opportunities as others. This stuck with you and as a result, being impartial and fighting for others to be treated fairly is not only meaningful but also fundamental to how you operate.

Prioritization: helping someone prioritize their wants and needs. You are fulfilled by helping others see that their wants and needs are a priority, because you know the pain of not having your needs prioritized.

Standing out: helping others not feel invisible. You are fulfilled by helping individuals or organizations stand out. This is connected to a core emotional challenge of feeling invisible. It's fulfilling for you to help others speak up and say what they are thinking.

Howard Schultz, CEO of Starbucks, Has a Clear Purpose

Howard Schultz, chairman and CEO of Starbucks, writes in his book, *Pour Your Heart into It*, that he was raised in a working-class Jewish family in Canarsie, Brooklyn, New York. While his mother Elaine tended to him and his siblings, his father Fred held a series of blue-collar positions, including truck driver, factory worker, and cab driver. In 1961, when Schultz was seven years old, his father broke his ankle. At the time, Fred had no health insurance or workers' compensation, and the family was left with no income. Schultz writes that he still remembers the way his father looked lying on the couch with his leg in a cast.

In a way, Schultz's tremendous professional success is a tribute to his father, who died years later, and as Schultz writes, "never attained fulfillment and dignity from work he found meaningful."

To me, it seems that Howard Schultz's core emotional challenge was seeing his family struggle, particularly when it came to their health. Throughout his career, Schultz's first priority has been his employees' well-being. Under his leadership, Starbucks began to offer every employee (including part-time workers) health insurance fairly early in the company's history. When this policy began in 1988, Starbucks was one of the first retail companies in the United States to offer part-time workers health insurance.[19]

Starbucks states on its website that its purpose is to share great coffee and help make the world a little better. This language is aligned with its mission: to inspire and nurture the human spirit— one person, one cup, and one neighborhood at a time. I've never met Howard Schultz, but I would wager that he is using his purpose to influence both his employees and his customers. Because he experienced the pain and burden of his parents not having health insurance or jobs that nurtured them, it's endlessly fulfilling for him to create the opposite for employees at Starbucks. There is no doubt that his high motivation is linked to fulfilling his purpose, and that it has become one of the key reasons Starbucks is such a success.

The Next Step

Now, let's put your purpose into action. In the next chapter, you will learn how to use your purpose to create more fulfillment at work, and you'll see just how often you are impacting others.

CHAPTER 5

FULFILLMENT = IMPACT

**Question: What does fulfillment
at work look like to you?**

Genius Action Plan: Measure Your Impact by
Assessing How Often You're Using Your Purpose

When I worked for Capital One, my colleagues and I would say regularly, "It's not like we're saving lives." This was how we articulated the lack of personal connection we felt to the impact of our work. I wasn't clear how what I did day to day impacted other people other than allowing them to have a credit card. I was in my twenties, I was achievement-driven, and finding fulfillment through my work didn't seem like a realistic goal.

This is not to say that a credit card company doesn't have

an impact. Giving someone a financial product that allows them to make purchasing decisions can be very empowering—it just wasn't something I related to on a deeply personal level. Now I know that the problem wasn't me or my job. I was just a poor fit because the impact the job had wasn't impactful to *me*: there was no connection to my purpose. Not everyone can save lives, but everyone deserves to feel that their work is contributing to something that's meaningful to them—in fact, it's crucial in order to reach the highest levels of success. If I had known then what I know now, I could have figured out a way to be more strategic with my genius and my purpose and sought out a job within the organization that was a better fit.

When I worked at Google, I felt even less fulfilled. Even though we had free food all day long, subsidized massages, game rooms, and the amazing Authors at Google talks that gave me access to some of the best thought leaders in the world, I wasn't engaged and knew I was in a job that wasn't right for me. I wasn't working within my Zone of Genius, and I was not making an impact that was meaningful to me. I didn't see how my work connected with anything important because I wasn't able to take the company's mission and connect it to my own.

Intrinsic Motivation versus Extrinsic Motivation

Intrinsic motivation refers to when you are engaging in an activity because it is rewarding in and of itself. At work, examples include:

- Volunteering to run a project because the work is aligned with your genius
- Creating a PowerPoint to help your colleagues understand a difficult concept that interests you
- Going for a promotion because the work excites you

In contrast, *extrinsic motivation* occurs when we are motivated to engage in an activity for the sole reason of earning a reward or avoiding punishment. At work, examples include:

- Completing a project in order to please your manager
- Working hard to close a deal in time to receive a bonus
- Going for a promotion just for the raise

When I was working at Google, I was suffering from a complete lack of intrinsic motivation. I was always trying to prove my worth, both to my manager and myself. When you don't feel motivated by the work you're doing, you have to cultivate your motivation using willpower, which is, unfortunately, the most common way people are motivated at work today. You know you are operating under these conditions when you wake up and have to push yourself out of bed and into the shower and then to your car, the subway, or the bus just to show up at work every day. This pattern causes stress and anxiety and the all-too-common burnout.

Some people say that this is just the way work is: we aren't supposed to leap out of bed with the feeling that we can't wait to start our day. I'm going to tell you now that those people are wrong. I don't believe we have to live this way, and I know for a fact that many others agree. In fact, most people, given the choice, want to work in a positive, fulfilling, and nurturing environment. As you learned in the last chapter, there is a real movement toward connecting work with purpose. This is particularly true for millennials, who now make up the majority of our workforce. According to Enso's World Value Index, 68 percent of millennials say creating change in the world is a personal goal that they actively pursue. Millennials are also known to choose experiences over material goods, so it's no surprise that they are more focused on purpose and impact than profits.

Purpose and impact are the fuel that keeps you going. They are what gets you up in the morning and your access to endless motivation and endless energy for the work you're doing. Just as Adam Grant has proven, if you know your impact,[20] your performance will improve, knowing the impact that is meaningful for you is information that will not only improve performance, but also connect you to your purpose.

WORKING WITH PURPOSE: MILLENNIALS AND BOOMERS

As a group, baby boomers and Gen X workers are more prone to ignore the inherent desire to work with purpose than millennials may be. This is one of the reasons why there is often a conflict between the youngest and the oldest generations in an office. Baby boomers view the younger generation as self-indulgent: they don't understand millennials' expectation to connect work with purpose.

At the same time, millennials view the boomers as sellouts, chasing profits over purpose. Gen Xers are caught in what the *New York Times* recently labeled "the grumpy middle." Gen Xers may want fulfillment but don't think they have the luxury to chase it in middle age.

The reality is that the business world is changing, and millennials' attitude seems to be that of the future. Connecting work with purpose is something that we all deserve and shouldn't sacrifice. We can't wait for retirement to do good because, even for the older generations, retirement isn't coming any time soon. People are living longer, and our lifestyles are more expensive than social security has planned for. If you're going to work well beyond your sixties, you need to love what you're doing, which is why knowing your purpose and your impact is essential.

Genius Action Plan: Measure Your Impact by Assessing How Often You're Using Your Purpose

Once you're clear on what your purpose is, and how you want to impact others, you can begin to assess how you can apply that to your work life.

Step One: Determine if your purpose is aligned with your company or organization. One way to figure that out is by looking at its mission and values statement. How does it express or communicate the impact the company wants to have on its customers?

Step Two: See if you can align your purpose to your company's mission statement. If so, it's likely that there is some aspect of the business that will provide intrinsic motivation for you. If you are interviewing with a new company, determine whether its daily actions reflect this mission statement by asking for specific examples from the people you're interviewing with. Unfortunately, lots of companies promote mission and values statements that are little more than window dressing. You'll want to make sure that any company you work for puts its money where its mouth is in regard to living up to their statement.

Companies are slowly realizing that to attract the best talent, they must be clear about their mission and their purpose for existing. This transparency about values and motivation makes choosing the right company for you easier, allowing you to align your purpose to the most forward-thinking organizations. While connecting to a company's mission statement doesn't guarantee that you're going to be happy at work, it can help you hone in on the impact the company is having and make sure that you can make a personal connection to it.

Microsoft's mission, for example, is "To empower every person and every organization on the planet to achieve more." When Satya Nadella became CEO in 2014, he made the creation of a new mission statement one of his first areas of focus. In June 2015, he sent a company-wide email, emphasizing the importance of this mission. He wrote, "Today, I want to share more on the overall context and connective tissue between our mission, worldview, strategy and culture... Our mission is to empower every person and every organization on the planet to achieve more. This mission is ambitious and at the core of what our customers deeply care about."

What I love about this statement is that Nadella is clear about what drives Microsoft, making it easy for current and prospective employees to see how they might connect their purpose to the organization's goals. This powerful mission statement could easily align with many of the personal purpose statements listed in chapter 4. If Microsoft is determined to help companies and people achieve more, each employee can figure out how they can contribute to that mission using their individual purpose statement.

Maximize Your Impact

Knowing the relationship between your purpose and the impact you make will provide you with the intrinsic motivation you are looking for. When you have endless motivation for your work, you will have the energy to achieve at a level you didn't think was possible. Yet so many people still see purpose as a nice-to-have and not an essential aspect of their work life. To make things easier, see if you can adopt one of these simple ways to gauge your impact within your organization.

Option One: You can gauge your impact by taking a close look at who you are working with. Depending on your job, those people might be your coworkers, your direct reports (if you are a manager), or your customers. Using the Performance Tracker, identify all the ways that you're impacting those around you. Look for patterns in your responses week over week. Are you having a consistent type of impact that is making a positive change to the company? Are the people around you responding or changing their behaviors based on your impact?

It's amazing how unaware we can sometimes be of our effect on others. I once had a friend who didn't realize until he left the company how powerful his impact was. His purpose was helping people collaborate and work well together. This work was extremely meaningful to him, and he helped people in this way all the time. He had always made a point to ensure that everyone on his team was working effectively, and he was often tapped to help resolve conflicts within other teams. It was obvious to everyone that he made a positive impact on others, but it didn't register with him how much he had made a difference to the organization. When he left the company to start his own business, he received dozens of emails from colleagues who all shared how much they enjoyed working with him and how strongly they felt his impact. In that moment he felt overwhelmed with a feeling of purpose. Imagine if he had recognized his impact sooner—he could have had that feeling of fulfillment every day. This is the importance of identifying your purpose and then making sure it's being leveraged as a tangible impact all the time.

Option Two: A second way of ensuring that you're making an impact is to track the moments when you feel fulfilled at work, using the Performance Tracker. When you notice yourself feeling emotionally connected with your work, pause and dissect the impact you're having in that moment. What is the impact that feels profound for you?

Building a Strategy for Maximizing Your Zone of Genius

Are you able to use your genius and have the impact that is connected to your purpose in your current job?

_____

_____

_____

_____

_____

What projects or areas of focus at work do you believe are in line with your genius?

_____

_____

_____

_____

_____

What are the key business objectives of your current role? What are the business objectives for your company this quarter and year?

_____

_____

_____

_____

_____

How can you connect your genius to your company's or team's business objectives?

_____

_____

_____

_____

_____

_____

What is your company's mission?

_____

_____

_____

_____

_____

How does this mission connect to your own purpose? Write a personal mission statement that connects your purpose to that of your company.

_____

_____

_____

_____

_____

_____

Hailey's Impact Improved Her Team

At just thirty-five years old, Hailey was the youngest marketing VP at a name-brand internet company. Although she loved the company and the product, she felt that there was something missing. She liked her job but didn't love it, and she didn't know why she wasn't more motivated to do her best. She was confident in her managing ability but felt that her team of three direct reports was not performing optimally: they were lagging behind developing new campaigns compared to another team in her department. This was particularly frustrating for Hailey because she was an ambitious person who believed that managing others was one of her strengths. She was also fast; her ability to get a lot done in a short amount of time was something that she believed made her stand out.

Hailey had struggled with schoolwork when she was young. She was never diagnosed, but she thinks she had a learning disability, because even though she worked hard she often had difficulty understanding the information she needed in order to complete her work. As she got older, Hailey realized that she needed more time to process information than others. As a result, she was a poor test taker and always a C+ student. The feeling that she was incapable of fully comprehending information was her core emotional challenge.

Not being able to understand her schoolwork didn't feel

good to Hailey, but she was never made to feel like it would prevent her from success. At home, Hailey was not punished for her mediocre grades, and her parents were extremely supportive. They would often tell her that she was "street smart" and talked about the importance of different types of intelligence, which helped Hailey build confidence. Her parents blamed the school system for instilling in her the belief that she wasn't A+ material.

I see this same core emotional challenge with many of my clients. They didn't perform well in school and now equate a lack of success to not being smart or valuable. When you are told from a young age that you're not good enough, it can impact your perception of your abilities for the rest of your life. In Hailey's case, she compensated for her learning difficulties by developing a vivacious personality and a strong and highly efficient work ethic. She was rewarded at work for being an energetic and effective leader, yet she was often switched from leading one team to another because her employees complained that they couldn't keep up with her. In fact, it was her fast pace that at times prevented her from fully explaining the scope of a project to her staff, which left them feeling confused and unmotivated. Her fast pace was something she viewed as an asset, but at times it left some of her colleagues questioning her judgment because she often made decisions without fully considering the potential outcomes.

Hailey's genius was her ability to think outside the box by taking on existing projects and making them better. We decided to call her genius Improvement Strategist. And clearly, her purpose was helping people *understand* the task at hand, because she would do anything to prevent others from feeling like they didn't have enough information to complete their work. Hailey told me that she felt the most fulfilled when she was helping other people understand the business and themselves. I explained to her that being more aware of her purpose would enable us to increase the amount of fulfillment she could experience at work, because she would be able to slow down and explain what she wanted from her team so that they could comprehend the task at hand.

I had Hailey use the Performance Tracker to record how often she was using her genius as well as her purpose, paying special attention to the impact questions. Within a few weeks of tracking her impact, she was able to see that she was helping her team comprehend assignments better once she slowed down. She spent extra time giving them updates on information that she, as a VP, was privy to, and made sure they were clear on what her expectations were. She also tracked how often she spent time getting to know her team better, and she shared the Performance Tracker with them so that they could understand themselves and their work habits. The Performance Tracker helped Hailey see that often, her behavior was getting in the way of creating the impact that was most meaningful to her. This was a light bulb moment. Her fast-paced working style was preventing her from using her purpose, both in her ability to feel like she was making a difference and in her effectiveness of giving others the information they needed to succeed. It became clear that her speed was preventing her from getting the full experience of fulfillment.

By taking the time to track her impact week over week, Hailey saw that her speed, which she had previously thought was one of her strengths, was also getting in the way of her fully experiencing her impact. When she slowed down, she was able to notice more nuance from her team and gain more fulfillment, because they understood her directions fully and performed at a higher level as a result.

The Performance Tracker showed Hailey exactly how her bad habits were preventing her from making the most impact at work. I explained to her that most people aren't paying attention to how they impact others, but once she could see it in action, she would experience fulfillment where she may have not expected to find it. Hailey was also able to identify specific performance issues that she hadn't noticed in herself before.

Because Hailey was a disciplined person and filled out the Tracker diligently for months, she was able to develop the Genius Habit quickly, and it stuck with her. She now tells me that she can almost unconsciously track her impact, which makes her feel more satisfied at work. What's more, she has fully embodied the mindfulness behaviors that allow her to be more in touch with herself, so that she can notice when she's going too fast and then purposefully slow down. Overall, she's more attuned with her performance and what is creating or preventing her best work. As a result of this increased awareness, Hailey has gotten more positive feedback from her managers and is making significant progress toward her goal of getting promoted.

Entering Your Zone of Genius: Combining Genius and Impact

Getting into your Zone of Genius is possible for everyone, and I promise it makes work exhilarating. In the ideal scenario, you use both your genius and purpose at work. It's like putting together a puzzle. You need to strategically create the work that will allow you to use your genius and then monitor the impact to confirm that you're fulfilling your purpose.

I like to describe it this way: you're in your Zone of Genius when you're using both your head and your heart. Your genius stems from the intellectual challenge and brain power necessary to do the work, and your purpose is driving the impact that fills your soul. When you're working within your Zone of Genius, you will feel fulfilled: you're making an impact that's meaningful to you, and even more powerfully, you feel that your work is your calling. When my clients are in their Zone of Genius, they describe it as feeling unstoppable. They also reach their career visions faster than they expect. They stop feeling drained by work, they are energized and excited about what they are doing, and they are constantly creating new and even more exciting opportunities to tackle.

Working within your Zone of Genius 100 percent of the time isn't realistic, but you can aim to use it often in your day-to-day life if you're conscious and proactive about it. Using the Performance Tracker is a great way to tell if you are actively creating opportunities that are right for you, and if not, provide the insight for you to course-correct quickly.

I strive to ensure that 70 percent of my workweek is spent doing work that is aligned with my Zone of Genius. The other 30 percent is work that I know I *have* to do; I know that it doesn't challenge me intellectually or have the impact that fulfills me, but it needs to get done. For me, work that doesn't fall within my Zone of Genius might be anything that is overly granular, like editing articles I've written or my business accounting. It's not terrible work and I know I have to do it, but it's not capitalizing on the strengths of my genius or fulfilling my purpose.

Amber Leveraged Her Genius to Reach the Next Level

When my client Amber first came to me, she was feeling ambivalent about her job. Amber was working for a marketing strategy consulting company and she enjoyed the people she worked with. She liked the work but often felt put upon: whenever a client was booked, the CEO would assign projects to team members as he saw fit, usually without asking if they wanted them or were available. Amber sensed that her level of fulfillment was not where it should be, that she should and could get more out of work. She just didn't know where to start.

We identified that Amber's genius was as an Innovative Process Strategist. Her ideal way of thinking was to create a structured process that solved a number of complex problems. For instance, she took it upon herself to create a system for tracking the organization's clients, because it was fun to do. She also created specific marketing processes that used data analytics to target potential customers. For her, creating these processes that improved how the whole business operated brought her pure delight.

Amber's purpose was to help individuals and businesses see their potential by revealing their authentic truths. Her core emotional challenge was feeling inadequate and not feeling seen for who she was. Amber told me that her family still judged the way she dressed, looked, and behaved. Her family was uncomfortable with the way she expressed her individuality and was constantly asking her to conform. Instead of feeling rebellious, she felt inadequate. As a result, she felt most fulfilled when she was helping others see themselves for who they were—something that I, as someone who struggles with a similar core emotional challenge, could definitely relate to!

For Amber, learning this information about herself was liberating. It immediately made her confidence surge because she not only felt like she was now clear on who she was, but she also saw the value of how it could affect her contributions at work. She started making an effort to ensure she was helping clients see their full potential, which helped them think bigger, as well as increased Amber's motivation and sense of purpose.

I was also able to help Amber see that her CEO was taking advantage of her inability to tell others when she was overloaded with work. While her CEO wasn't singling her out and treated many employees the same way, she had a particularly difficult time telling him how she felt. Amber had a habit of saying yes to everything that was asked of her. By taking on every task that was handed to her, she often ended up doing work that was boring or didn't play to her strengths. Once she understood her genius and her purpose, it gave her the license to say no. In fact, she immediately started gracefully turning down assignments that were not aligned with her genius. Because she had put a lot of thought into what kind of work she was most effective at, she was able to explain why certain projects would be better assigned to other team members. As a result, her CEO was able to assign her projects that challenged her in the best way possible—and her results soon spoke for themselves.

Amber didn't stop there. Within a few months of identifying her Zone of Genius, she decided she wanted to start her own marketing consulting company, rewrote her vision for her life and career, and set about creating it. She became an entrepreneur and was loving running her own business until one of her clients offered her a full-time job, which she accepted. Amber was open to making the jump from running her own business to working for someone else because the opportunity was perfectly aligned with her Zone of Genius and would take her career to the next level. She reported to me recently that the new job has in fact been everything she had hoped it would be, and she is already re-envisioning her career with loftier goals. Knowing her, she's on her way to achieving them sooner than even she thinks is possible.

TAKING THE GENIUS HABIT HOME

You can function within your Zone of Genius outside of work; in fact, it can be applied to every aspect of your life. Understanding your Zone of Genius affects the way you relate and react to everything and everyone, because it allows you to look at your life through a specific lens that emphasizes your strengths across a variety of situations. The result is that you can make better decisions that are more aligned with who you really are. Whether it's figuring out how to approach challenges in your personal relationships, engaging in exercise or hobbies, or starting up a side hustle, you may be surprised to find that the methods of consciously engaging your genius, addressing your core emotional challenge, and tracking your activities can be enormously helpful outside the office. If your job doesn't allow you to engage your genius as much as you would like, bringing the Genius Habit home is a great way to practice those skills and prepare for the time when you will be able to use them more at work.

Think about how you can bring the Genius Habit to your daily life. How will it inform your personal relationships? Can you use it to increase your level of engagement? In my life, I use the Genius Habit to keep track of my interactions with my partner so I can make sure I'm having the impact I desire on our relationship. The bottom line is that understanding your Zone of Genius and making it a habit to engage with it regularly can help guide you create more enjoyable moments in all aspects of your life.

Anyone Can Experience Purpose and Impact

We are inundated with Instagram messages and retweets of the "find your purpose" variety every day, yet so many of us struggle to execute on it. I can't tell you how many times I have seen quotes from famous, successful people shared on Facebook or framed and put on someone's desk, yet the person sharing it or displaying the quote honestly doesn't know how to use the advice in his or her own life. The intention of this chapter has been to show you that your purpose matters and to give you the tools to put it into action. The next time you read a repost of Oprah's famous quote, "Everybody has a calling. And your real job in life is to figure out as soon as possible what that is, who you were meant to be, and to begin to honor that in the best way possible for yourself," you won't think she's just trying to inspire you.[21] You will have a deep understanding of what she's talking about, because you'll be doing it every day.

While we all can't expect to have (and many of us don't desire) the kind of extraordinary public success and fame that Oprah has experienced, the more you stay aligned with your genius and purpose, the more likely you are to experience the kind of success that aligns with *your* vision for your life and career.

Think about Your Purpose and Impact

At this point, I hope you've gleaned some interesting insights about yourself, including your core emotional challenge. If you've recognized it, can you see how it may be affecting your work? More importantly, can you flip it on its head and see how you can make a real and lasting impact on others by engaging with your purpose? Here are a few further questions to consider:

- What is the impact on others that you've had in your life up until now? How do you feel about that?
- Now that you know your purpose, how can you begin to create more fulfillment in your day-to-day life?
- Are you ready to start making fulfillment a priority?

The Next Step: Three Key Performance Behaviors

Throughout the rest of the book, you will learn about the three behaviors you must cultivate in order to fully use your genius and purpose and achieve your ultimate career experience: joy, mindfulness, and perseverance. Regardless of what your genius or purpose is, these are the muscles that you must exercise and build in order to achieve extraordinary levels of success.

PART III

JOY

CHAPTER 6

STOP EQUATING ACHIEVEMENTS WITH HAPPINESS

Question: Are you an achievement junkie?

Genius Action Plan: Focus on the
Process, Not the Outcome

One of the ways that our education system is no longer aligned with the culture of the business world is that it doesn't teach us how to self-motivate or tap into our internal drive in addition to achieving goals. Instead, we've been taught to wait to be told what to do and recycle information that has been spoon-fed to us. In the past, this wasn't as much of a problem for many workers, because the business world mirrored our education system: as an employee, you were told what to do, and if you didn't understand the task, you looked to your manager for direction.

This way of thinking also applied to career advancement: ask someone more knowledgeable for advice and follow their lead. You slowly moved up the corporate ladder, and you knew that if you worked hard and stuck it out for many years, you would rise to the top.

However, in today's fast-paced, competitive market, businesses are seeking ideas and answers to problems that require thinking that is entirely different than "business as usual." Yet our education hasn't prepared us with the skills the working world now requires, such as problem-solving, taking initiative, and proactively managing our own job performance and, in the bigger picture, our careers. There is no longer a slow, inevitable crawl up the corporate ladder. Instead, if you want to get ahead, you must rely on your own motivation and drive. You have to generate hunger within yourself and proactively navigate toward the work that is aligned with your genius and purpose by owning the process of creating work that excites and fulfills you. Only you can create the life and career you want.

It's clear that we live and work in a goal-oriented, achievement-based world in which we're told that job satisfaction comes from winning, in much the same way that you strived for good grades in school or wins on the sports field. But here's the thing: while winning is always exciting, it's nothing more than a momentary victory. Yesterday's win will not sustain your enthusiasm for your job for more than a few days. After the euphoria of achievement wears off, you start to look for another goal to achieve so you can experience that feeling again.

If you're able to focus on enjoying the process of work, not simply accomplishing individual goals, you'll be able to get more out of your everyday experience and find your job to be more fulfilling. And the key to getting to that point of enjoying the process is working within your Zone of Genius. That's also the place where you're going to be able to transcend the level of success you're used to experiencing and get bigger results than you may have even thought possible.

Take Warren Buffett, for example, who demonstrates the behavior of someone who is clearly working within his Zone of Genius. He loves his job of running Berkshire Hathaway so much that in his late eighties he has no intention of quitting anytime soon. As he says, he "tap dances his way to work." The fact that Buffett has accumulated so much wealth yet doesn't care much for spending is a clear sign that he loves the process of his work just as much as, if not more than, the outcome of earning billions. In the HBO documentary *Becoming Warren Buffett*, it's clear that he built a business that aligned perfectly with his genius. Buffett is obsessed with the concept of compound interest, so I would wager that his genius has something to do with creating growth opportunities. He is challenged by taking investments and growing them as fast as possible, and compound interest is one of his tools. These are clear indications that he is challenged—in the best way possible—by his work, and as a result he couldn't be happier.

Roger Ebert is another famous example of someone who knew his genius and leveraged it for incredible success. In the documentary of his career, *Life Itself*, he talked about "being in the zone" when he was writing while battling cancer. He said, "When I am writing, my problems become invisible, and I am the same person I always was. All is well. I am as I should be."[22] Ebert's many extraordinary achievements did not compare, in his mind, to his love of the writing process. Although he became one of the most successful movie critics of all time, to him, he was just doing what he loved and what he was good at. This is the absolute return you get by avoiding the trappings of the achievement junkie path.

If you don't tap into your genius and enjoy the process of work, you aren't really maximizing your potential—you're living for the temporary wins. The key is to distinguish between the enjoyment and challenge we get from operating in our Zone of Genius and overdosing on achievement.

Achievement Junkies

Many people are what I refer to as achievement junkies. They believe that the act of achievement makes them happy, because something achieved is a sign that they've met a goal: closed a deal, got a promotion, landed a prestigious job title, etc. Achievement junkies constantly reserve their excitement for the moment that they achieve something and grind through the work it takes to get to those moments. Depending on the type of achievement that person is striving for, they might not be rewarded more often than every few weeks, months, or sometimes years. That's not the experience of having real joy at work, and, despite what many people think, it's not the path to extraordinary success.

Some achievement junkies have certainly become successful (depending on your definition of success), attaining wealth beyond measure. But I would bet they're not prioritizing their health or their relationships. It's probable that every other aspect of their life is suffering in some way because maintaining the lifestyle required to land high-level achievements all the time when you don't enjoy the process of the work is stressful and requires an enormous amount of effort. To me, those achievements are cheap versions of what can be attained through understanding your genius and purpose. And anyone who says "My purpose is making more money" doesn't really understand the science of motivation.

According to Alfie Kohn, who wrote in the *Harvard Business Review*:

> Incentives, a version of what psychologists call extrinsic motivators, do not alter the attitudes that underlie our behaviors. They do not create an enduring commitment to any value or action. Rather, incentives merely—and

temporarily—change what we do. As for productivity, at least two dozen studies over the last three decades have conclusively shown that people who expect to receive a reward for completing a task or for doing that task successfully simply do not perform as well as those who expect no reward at all.[23]

This information may seem surprising. Of course, money, the most obvious extrinsic reward, is necessary to buy the things people want and need. Many businesses have bought into the idea that rewards motivate people, which is why many companies that are seeking great talent use the dangling carrot of endless perks to secure new hires. Like other companies in Silicon Valley, Google is especially known for going overboard on the free perks. I loved those perks when I worked there; in fact, they kept me in a job that wasn't right for me longer than I might have otherwise stayed. But did the superficial benefits motivate me to give my all and do my best work? No. That is the problem with extrinsic rewards: they hook you, but they don't motivate you. According to a *Time* magazine interview with Daniel Pink, "Rewards just motivate people to get more rewards, and when the rewards go away, people stop. And if you want anything other than basic manual labor—if you want creative work or analytical work—rewards can actually backfire."[24]

Achievement junkies stake their happiness on the energizing

feeling they get at the moment of scoring an extrinsic reward. If you are hanging your happiness on achievements, you have to continually be striving to achieve—which, in the world of work, quickly becomes exhausting and unsustainable.

Most achievement junkies I encounter will tell me that they like their job, but when I press them, I discover that what they really like is achieving goals. The actual process of their work, not to mention their genius and purpose, is not taken into consideration. This is why so many seemingly successful people are stressed, close to burnout, and sleep-deprived. When you don't enjoy the process of your work, you have to consistently use willpower to keep going, which drains your energy, versus being driven by an internal desire, which is energizing.

Worst of all, even though it might be stressful, it's easy to become an achievement junkie. Social media has made it even easier to fall into this trap. According to Mauricio Delgado, associate professor of psychology at Rutgers University, you get two dopamine hits when you post about an accomplishment online: one from the achievement itself and the second from sharing it with your friends.

It's also easier to talk about specific achievements than about general fulfillment, because achievements are concrete and easy to explain. When was the last time someone said to you, "Wow, I had such a great week at work! I'm loving the process of this project I am working on." The more standard conversation is

"Wow, I had such a great week at work! I nailed a presentation and brought in two new clients." The trouble is, it's not always possible to hit a big goal every week. So what sustains you when your big achievements are few and far between?

My answer is to choose being in the zone over being an achievement junkie. While anyone can reach a goal or have an achievement, not everyone takes the time to find work that is truly fulfilling and energizing on a deeper level. Just as any unhealthy habit won't make you happier in the long term, working only for the goal of achievements will limit your potential and likely make your life miserable in the meantime.

When you put your achievement junkie tendency in check, you can be just as energized and excited about doing the work that's in front of you every day as you might formerly have been about achieving a goal. Once you start using the Performance Tracker, you will be tracking how much you are enjoying or not enjoying the process of your daily work. This will also help you see how often you are focusing on the achievements. The key is to pay attention to the process of your work and whether you're using your genius. By course-correcting and using your genius more in your everyday tasks, you will start to see the difference between enjoying the process and not. Achievements are always fun to have, of course, but instead of being the only source of enjoyment, when you're operating within your genius, you'll be enjoying the rest of your job as well.

How I Kicked the Achievement Junkie Habit

I admit, I was an achievement junkie. Getting jobs at Capital One and then Google was my first set of achievements and proved to me that I could be successful in the world—at least in terms of the way our society often defines success. During the time I worked at each company, the achievements I was chasing were the goals that were set for me to reach or the feeling of accomplishment I felt when I finished a project. At the time, I hadn't identified my Zone of Genius, and I didn't even imagine that it was possible to love nearly all the work that I did every day. At the same time, I also struggled with fatigue, stress, frustration, and sometimes depression, and the occasional fleeting feeling of happiness when I got one of those dopamine hits. Because I didn't know any better, I simply accepted that these feelings about work were as good as it was going to get.

It wasn't until I started building my own business that I got a taste of loving work every day. I've never looked back. Now I enjoy the process of my work, sometimes even *more* than achieving goals. Because I have sought out work that allows me to use my genius and have the impact of my purpose every day, I'm intrinsically motivated and able to tap into endless sources of pure energy I didn't previously know I had. As a result, work has become something that is part of me. It's not something that I try to turn off on Fridays, and I no longer think of it as a job; I think of my work as a calling. Achieving goals reminds me that I am on the right path, but it doesn't define my journey—and I wouldn't have it any other way.

SUSTAINED HAPPINESS AND PERFORMANCE

You may think that being happy at work is nothing more than a nice-to-have, but happiness can be a powerful—and maybe even crucial—tool for success. For those doubters who still think that grinding through daily work and focusing on extrinsic rewards is not that bad, I can tell you that a lack of enjoyment and happiness will eventually affect your performance. It turns out, happiness is an important ingredient for success. Shawn Anchor, author of *The Happiness Advantage*, found that a happier brain works much more efficiently, is more creative, and is better at solving problems. When workers are happy, they're more effective collaborators, which I've mentioned is integral in today's business environment.

Companies that invest in helping their employees be happier are more successful. In Dr. Noelle Nelson's book, *Make More Money by Making Your Employees Happy*, she explains, "When employees feel that the company takes their interest to heart, then the employees will take company's interests to heart." Nelson cites a study from the Jackson Organization, a survey research consultancy, that shows that companies that work to enhance an employee's feeling of value enjoy a return on equity and assets more than *triple* that experienced by firms that don't. The study went on to point out that the stock prices of companies listed on *Fortune's* 100 Best Companies to Work For rose an average of 14 percent per year from 1998 through 2005, compared to 6 percent for the overall market.

Being in the zone ensures that you're loving the process, enjoying what you do, and feeling fulfilled, increasing the likelihood that you're happy. All of these benefits are the precursors to having big ideas, being innovative, and, yes, achieving the kind of far-reaching impact that Warren Buffett and Roger Ebert have experienced.

Negative Thoughts Sabotage Your Ability to Perform

The logic of the achievement junkie is a vicious cycle: if you're only getting your enjoyment from achieving a goal, you have to achieve that goal in order to be happy. In this scenario, you're actually creating a threatening environment for yourself: every time you miss a deadline or don't achieve the goal, you beat yourself up and consider yourself a failure. According to Ashley Merryman and Po Bronson, authors of *Top Dog: The Science of Winning and Losing*, the stress that comes with a threatening environment can negatively affect your performance. Their book features a study in which researchers presented students at Princeton University with a list of GRE questions. For half the students, the questions were presented in a threatening context—they were a test of the students' ability, a judgment on whether they truly belonged at Princeton. The other students received the same questions, but in a challenging context, where they were encouraged to try their best and didn't have a judgment attached to their outcome. Their version of the test was titled "Intellectual Challenge Questionnaire," and the questions were construed as brainteasers. In the threat context, the Princeton undergrads got 72 percent of the questions correct. In the challenge context, an equally talented group got 90 percent correct.[25] The takeaway here is that in a challenge state, you're not exerting energy worrying about the outcome, so you can focus on doing your best. Based on this knowledge, creating a threat situation by being focused on the achievement greatly impacts your ability to perform.

Think about how often we create threat situations for ourselves at work: we worry we will be fired for missing a sales target; we think that our performance on a presentation dictates our value; we assume that our colleagues' success makes us look like failures in comparison. We unconsciously think that if we create worry or fear, we are being more careful and calculated, but the truth is exactly the opposite—you are actually sabotaging your ability to perform at your best. Reframing work by creating a challenge versus a threat environment will actually help you achieve more. And doing so can be as simple as giving yourself the mental space to shift your perspective.

The Curse of the Golden Handcuffs

So many people are stressed-out achievement junkies, and they think that's the way work is supposed to make them feel. If you asked them, they would probably say that they're not that happy at work but wouldn't do anything to change it. They believe their discontent is the price they pay for their expensive lifestyle or the external rewards they're receiving. They may also worry that by changing the situation they will lose their job security or the paycheck that allows them to buy the things they think provide happiness. This cycle of staying in a job you don't like just for a big paycheck is often referred to as the *golden handcuffs*. I think it can also describe many people who fear the loss of security or a consistent paycheck and allow that fear to be the priority over their happiness. I know these experiences all too well. When I didn't love work, the things I bought with my paycheck seemed more important than my actual job. But when I had to give them up to make the shift into the entrepreneurial work I do now, the tangible trappings of my life no longer held much importance. That's when I realized that I was attaching my happiness to stuff I could buy, rather than associating it directly with my work. Now that I'm fully engaged in work that has a huge impact on others and challenges me every day, I no longer need the shopping spree.

Tabitha Was an Achievement Junkie

My client Tabitha is a great example of an achievement junkie in a job that created a threatening environment. She worked in sales, and she was tremendously stressed out at the end of every quarter because if she didn't meet her numbers, she and her whole team would be called out as not meeting expectations. There would then be extra pressure put on them for the next quarter. She knew that she wouldn't be fired for missing her numbers once, but if it became a pattern, her ability to get promoted or stay in the job was at risk. Tabitha was so focused on making her numbers that the achievement began to define her. She often couldn't sleep through the night, and she was anxious all the time.

When I first met with Tabitha, I explained to her what was happening with her body. Stress increases the amount of cortisol we produce, which constricts your blood vessels and prevents you from operating optimally.[26] It puts you into the well-known fight, flight, or freeze mode, which means you're not thinking clearly, and ultimately affects performance. She was not only stressed to the max, but she also wasn't showing up at work healthy and ready to go. Her reaction? Push harder, sleep less, and work more hours. It was almost like she was a time bomb, waiting to explode.

I helped Tabitha realize that if she was getting stressed to the point where she couldn't sleep, it was possible that she may be in the wrong job. I explained that sales is an area of business often filled with achievement junkies, but there are also people who love the art of the sale. Those are the ones who get their numbers not because of the dangling carrot, but because they enjoy the process, and the work allows them to use their strengths in a way that is meaningful to them. Their genius is usually in talking to people and building relationships. The actual sale is the cherry on top.

The sales process actually matched Tabitha's Zone of Genius perfectly. She was a Collaboration Strategist, which meant she felt challenged and energized when she was bringing people together in order to solve a problem. In her sales role, she was building relationships for the purpose of helping new and existing clients solve a particular problem, and she found this part of the job challenging and invigorating. Her purpose was making others feel accepted for being who they are, and she used this purpose often with her internal team. She felt that she was able to get the impact that was fulfilling to her by helping her team feel good about being who they were and showing them how to approach their work from their genius strengths. Yet the environment of a sales team accentuated her achievement junkie tendency. So, while the thinking and problem-solving were a good fit for her, the environment was not.

We discussed endless ways Tabitha could apply her Zone of Genius to her career, with sales being just one option. I believed that her current department was not the best fit, given the fact that the high-pressure environment elevated her stress levels and was detrimental to her ability to enjoy life. I explained to her that great performance is a combination of knowing and operating in your Zone of Genius, as well as finding the right environment that allows you to be joyful. Tabitha worked for a company that valued its employees, which meant transferring to another department within the company was always an option. I suggested that a job that didn't involve meeting quarterly targets might be a better fit for her, and we talked about positions in the company that were more project-based and management-focused, which would allow her to enjoy herself and be healthier. In the end, Tabitha decided to stay in her sales job, but she started to think more seriously about changing departments. Just knowing that there were other options within her organization that would allow her to be less stressed created an interesting effect—she felt more relaxed.

Are You an Achievement Junkie?

Answer the following questions to gain insight about how you perceive your work most of the time:

1. Your excitement for your job comes primarily from accomplishing goals, winning deals, or anything that is related to an achievement; the work process for getting to that achievement is not that enjoyable.

   YES
   NO

2. Work is only fun when you're achieving goals.

   YES
   NO

3. When you think of the future, you think in terms of what more you can achieve rather than what fulfills and challenges you.

   YES
   NO

4. You often get bored with the work you're doing.

   YES
   NO

5. You struggle to feel fulfilled or intellectually challenged by your job.

   YES
   NO

If you answered yes to four or five of the above questions, you're an achievement junkie. The problem is that at some point you will burn out because you are not challenged or fulfilled by the work you're doing. It's likely that you already have to motivate yourself using your own willpower, which is not an optimal way to operate. You may feel exhausted or stressed out at work.

If you answered yes to two or three questions, you may have achievement junkie tendencies. You might enjoy some aspects of your work but not others. To increase your success, it will be important to examine your ability to increase your access to the enjoyable parts of your job. If you aren't able to do that in your current position, it might be time to look for another role. By taking action you will avoid burnout, or worse, getting fired for being in a job that isn't the right fit for you.

If you answered with zero or one yes response, you're not an achievement junkie. Congratulations! That means you are enjoying the hits of dopamine that you get from achievements but recognize that the short-lived high is just one aspect of a job you love, not the only excitement you're getting out of your work. You are actively working within your Zone of Genius, which means you are enjoying the process of achieving your goals as much as the actual achievement of them. This is the ideal place to be. Keep doing what you're doing!

Tom and Kate Never Found Joy at Work

Tom and Kate are two of my clients who are both achievement junkies. They don't know each other, but they have a lot in common. To anyone looking in from the outside, they both appear successful. In each of their offices, they are considered superstars.

Kate is a senior executive at a technology company, and Tom reports directly to the CEO of a small company. They both make good money, have a great lifestyle, and keep getting promoted. Yet, despite their apparent success, neither Tom nor Kate is happy. Tom never experiences any in-the-zone moments at work. Instead, he struggles with anxiety and signs of burnout. He is convinced that if he just works harder, he can be happy in his job. Kate wakes up in the middle of the night and can't go back to sleep because she's thinking about and dreading everything she has to do the next day.

When I ask each of them what fulfills them at work, they both mention hitting their targets and accomplishing goals. Kate and Tom both struggle to understand the concept of the Genius Habit because they are conditioned to believe that work satisfaction is associated only with accomplishments.

When Tom and Kate each hired me to help them find more career satisfaction, I told them that enjoying work was possible, but it would involve completely rewiring how they oriented themselves toward work. They would need to learn how to enjoy the process of their work more than the achievements. I could show them how to do this, but the choice of making that change was up to them.

Tom decided that it was worth a shot. He truly wanted to be happy. We worked through the Performance Tracker to see if we could reframe his orientation to work. Could he enjoy the process as much as achieving the goal? While his intentions were good, Tom kept falling back on prioritizing individual goals. He continually allowed himself to get pulled into an absurd workload, yet he would complain that he felt he needed to do it in order to get ahead. The idea that work should be joyless was rooted too deeply for Tom to accept the idea of the Genius Habit. He didn't believe he could be successful unless he was constantly overworked and achieving goals. His stress continued to be a problem, but he felt powerless to change.

Kate knew that the culture of her organization wasn't a great fit for her, but she wasn't willing to take the risk of leaving and making less money. Even with all of her complaining, using the Performance Tracker, and my coaching, she chose to stay in a job that caused her endless frustration. Every time she expressed dissatisfaction with her job, her company would offer her another raise. Her achievement junkie tendencies kept her in a job that wasn't right but rewarded her anyway.

Both Tom and Kate's stories illustrate how hard it is to shake the achievement junkie habit, but that doesn't mean you can't do it. It just takes effort and a whole new mind-set. My client Peter had a totally different experience when he put aside his achievement junkie tendencies and focused on using his genius. Peter is one of the most driven and ambitious of all my clients. He is uber-competitive: in college he was drafted to be a professional baseball player. When Peter and I met for the first time, I knew he was going to be the perfect client. His drive for maximizing his potential was just as high as his drive to succeed.

Peter came to me when he had taken what he thought was his dream job, as the CEO of a small company. He told me, "This is what I have always wanted, and I want to make sure I can do this job well." We started working together so that I could help him bring his Zone of Genius into his daily work. But within a few weeks we discovered that what he thought was his dream job was actually just his achievement junkie tendencies in action. He wanted to be at the top, but we realized that being a CEO didn't allow him to use his genius (Opportunity Evangelist) as often as he wanted, because he wasn't able to spend a large portion of his time looking for ways to take the company to the next level by finding lucrative opportunities, via either sales or finding investors. He believed he needed to focus on the areas of running a business that he wasn't naturally good at. As a result, he found himself not enjoying the position he had been chasing for so long.

Peter loved to make business deals, and it was the perfect arena for using his genius. Keeping this information in mind, we used the Performance Tracker and focused on tracking his enjoyment of (or lack of) the process of work. This meant that we weren't just focusing on how many deals he made each week, but the percentage of time when he was doing tasks that he didn't enjoy. I explained to Peter that the times when he was working outside of his genius were exactly when he reverted to being outcome-focused. What we discovered was that Peter was spending 80 percent of his time managing work that wasn't aligned with his genius and that he wasn't particularly effective at executing. We also worked on shifting his thinking. Rather than spend his time on areas that didn't play to his strengths, we discussed how he could leverage others to focus on them. As a leader he had the ability to delegate; he just didn't think he should. I suggested that Peter strive to work within his Zone of Genius 70 percent of the time and reserve 30 percent of his time for checking off mundane tasks and things that needed to get done but weren't necessarily aligned with his strengths. This way he could avoid getting spread too thin and reducing his overall impact. I have found the 70/30 mix to be manageable for many of my clients—and it's often a huge improvement for people who were previously spending the majority of their time on work that wasn't aligned with their genius and purpose.

The sooner you can identify where you're spending your time, the sooner you can make changes to shift your workload toward your Zone of Genius. Proactively managing your time versus being at the mercy of your calendar is also a behavior that is linked with great leadership. You can't lead when you're stretched too thin, and the most effective leaders play to their strengths and delegate the work that doesn't. This style of leadership gives other people the opportunity to shine and allows the organization to benefit from a leader doing what they're best at. Those leaders that try to be the jack of all trades end up struggling to find the time to really lead.

If you don't have the ability to control which projects or tasks you work on, identify ways for you to shift the balance of your tasks to better engage your genius a larger percent of the time. Just like my client Miranda did in chapter 3, you can offer up your unique perspective whenever the opportunity arises. Your natural way of problem-solving or thinking is probably needed more often than you think. When it comes to using your genius, be bold.

Peter decided to reinvent his role so that it better fit him. Because he was a CEO, he had the ability to leverage others to do the work that wasn't aligned with his genius, and he was able to decide which tasks he wanted to focus on and which ones he would assign to others on his team. Although most people don't work at the CEO level, I have found that everyone, no matter their level of seniority, has more power over managing their time and work than they realize.

Today, Peter spends most of each day making deals that will help his company grow. He focuses on finding clients via deal-making or by securing financing from investors. As a result of the reinvention of his role, Peter is less stressed out, he loves his work, and he still achieves his goals. He discovered that work can be a win-win. You can enjoy the process and, by tapping into the skills and mind-set that engage your genius, improve your performance.

Think about Replacing Achievement with Joy

Coming to terms with your identity as an achievement junkie can be overwhelming, but the truth is that most of your colleagues are likely in the same boat. It's not your fault that you've been trained to focus on goals and achievements in your professional life. However, you can break out of this stressful cycle and begin to relish the process of work, not just the outcome. Think about the following questions:

1. Do you believe that you deserve to find joy in your work every day? If you believe you're not capable of finding work that you enjoy or that you don't deserve joy, or you don't think work that is enjoyable for you exists, think again. Your negative mind-set is holding you back.

2. Can you pinpoint the time in your life where you picked up your achievement junkie habit?

Genius Action Plan: Focus on the Process, Not the Outcome

Achievement junkie or not, you can always prioritize enjoyment. It's as simple as focusing on the process of your work. Try to separate yourself from the outcome of your work and ask yourself, *Do I enjoy the process of the different tasks that I'm doing at work?*

If you don't, that's another sign that the Genius Habit could be a game changer for you. In fact, disliking the process of your work is a cue to pull out your Performance Tracker ASAP and get clear on how you can start using your genius more.

The Next Step

My hope at this point in your journey is that you are starting to know yourself better and can see how behaviors you have learned from society may be subverting your ability to either enjoy your work life or achieve greatness. The good news is that these bad habits are all fixable if you pay attention to the details of your daily life. The next step is to see if the guidance you're getting from your mentor or others really matches how you envision your future.

CHAPTER 7

DITCH YOUR MENTOR

Question: Are you relying on others to make career decisions for you?

Genius Action Plan: Filter Advice and Support through Your Zone of Genius

When I first meet many of my clients, they often ask me to give them solutions to their problems. They want to know exactly what they should do to get a promotion, which job offer should they consider, how to climb the ladder at their company, or how to create a plan for them to meet a five-year goal. When I tell them that they already have the ability to answer these questions, they are always skeptical. The typical response I get is, "Laura, that's the problem. I don't know *how* to do that."

I know we're all capable of crafting a career path that will lead us to success. But I also know that there are many people who are so unhappy in their current roles that they can't see the path even if it's right in front of them. Instead, our default has become to rely on others to tell us what to do, how to think, and who to be, especially when it comes to something enormous and over-whelming like building a career.

Because of these deeply ingrained habits, it's no wonder that many career decisions today are more often than not made based on what others think. We are all too eager to solicit advice and take it, even if we know in our hearts that the recommendation may not be right. There are countless ways to rationalize follow-ing a suggested career move that isn't the right fit: the salary is significant, a job looks good on the resume, you would be fol-lowing the same plan that worked for your brother, sister, father, friend, etc.

It's time we stop worrying about what other people tell us and listen instead to ourselves. Your genius and your purpose can guide you to decisions that will work for you, but only if you filter out the rest of the noise coming from the outside.

Tapping into your innate ability to determine what is right for you, and then ensuring your decisions are aligned with your genius and purpose, is key to experiencing joy and success at work on an ongoing basis. Knowing yourself, following your instincts and intuition, and confidently approaching decisions with clarity will bring you both peace of mind and something even more valuable—a career that is absent of regrets.

If you are having trouble deciding your career path, it's OK to ask for advice or support. In this chapter, though, I'm going to teach you how to take newly gleaned information for what it is: advice, not a road map or a mandate. And who should you turn to when you're seeking that advice? Let's start with your mentor.

Do I Really Need a Mentor?

A near-universal rule in business is that having a mentor or someone to regularly ask for advice is beneficial for your career. Some people believe that if you don't have a mentor, you may be missing out on a critical piece of the success formula. I don't exactly buy into this logic.

First, let's get clear on who a mentor could be and what role they might play in your career development. A mentor is usually an unpaid volunteer who supports your career. In big companies, the role might even be assigned as a leadership opportunity, allowing executives to offer their time to guide employees.

Mentors can actually be anyone. It could be someone in the same field that you have a third-party connection with, perhaps a friend of a friend or someone you meet when networking. This is why for many people starting their careers, it's not easy to go out and find a mentor. More often than not, the relationship develops organically, and an offer originates from the mentor who is expressing a desire to help the mentee. When these organic relationships do occur, it can feel magical. Who wouldn't want a high-powered individual to volunteer their time to help them? If Oprah Winfrey offered to be my mentor, rest assured, I would be delighted beyond measure.

I have always wanted to have a true mentor but have struggled to find one. Instead, I have experienced instances of someone offering to do something really meaningful to help me, more like a one-time favor. I can easily come up with a handful of times when people supported me in ways that were extremely helpful at different points in my career. When those moments occurred, I was grateful beyond belief. Yet I have never had a real mentor, someone I could count on over the course of many months or years. As a result, I have learned that just like almost any career tool, a mentor is nice to have but not a necessity for success. My career has not suffered as a result of not having a long-term mentor, and yours doesn't need to either.

Other people I have interviewed have credited much of their success to certain mentors, validating the idea that it can be a rewarding and essential part of some people's success formula. The key is not beating yourself up if you don't have one. If you do find someone who is willing to take on that role and who you think would be a perfect fit, approach the relationship with confidence and gratitude. Just remember that having a mentor is not a guarantee for career success—it's just another tool that, if used wisely, can be a huge source of support as you chart your path.

WHAT MAKES A MENTOR RELATIONSHIP WORK

I once had the opportunity to work with a mentor from a company called Everwise. Everwise works like a matchmaker: it connects volunteer mentors to those who need one. They go into a company and match employees with their cadre of volunteer mentors, or they facilitate mentor relationships within the organization. At the time, I needed someone who was well versed in the software industry and could help me think through a long-term vision for a partnership with a certain software company. I was matched with someone who had the exact experience I was looking for. We limited our discussions to the topic I needed guidance on, and we had a very successful, structured, and short relationship. But after I received the information and help I needed, we parted ways. I didn't view the relationship as a long-standing endeavor or one in which we would discuss the overall path of my career. In the end, I got exactly what I wanted and needed out of that short-term mentor relationship, and I was grateful.

I've also known people who had mentors that really disappointed them. For some, the disappointment stemmed from confusion about who was driving the process or should create a clear structure or set of expectations. As a result, the conversations weren't concise, and the value of the relationship was hard to pinpoint. Others have struggled to incorporate their mentor's advice into their careers. The relationship crumbled because the mentor was giving advice that didn't resonate, and the mentee didn't execute it, thereby removing the motivation for the mentor's involvement. It's crucial that the relationship is a good fit for both parties and that everyone has clear expectations of the goals they are working toward. The experience needs to be mutually beneficial; otherwise, everyone loses interest.

How to Identify the Right Mentor

The way people approach relationships with mentors is where they often lose themselves. When you ask someone to be your mentor, make sure they are a good fit for you, your genius, and your career objectives by asking these questions:

- What is your mentor's background and how does their experience pertain to yours? Unless the mentor is a trained career coach, advice they give may be a regurgitation of their own experience, which may or may not be applicable to your situation.

- Are they able to be completely objective? Ideally, a mentor is someone who is not affected by your decisions and is a source of unbiased advice. If the mentor is a friend of the family, it would be hard for them not to suggest ideas that would benefit your family as a whole, versus suggesting something that is right just for you.

- Is there an end point to this relationship? With mentors working in a volunteer capacity, it's a good practice to discuss how long you're going to be meeting together to show you value the mentor's time and don't want to take advantage of it.

- Is there a mutual benefit? Make sure that both parties are clear about their intentions and that everyone involved is getting something positive from the time spent together. Often mentors are leveraging their purpose by helping others, so it's good to hear from them why they're willing to do the work.

- What are your goals? As the mentee, it's always good to be clear with the mentor what your goals are and what you need from them. This is especially important if the mentor is actually someone with a high profile, as it can be intimidating to communicate clearly to someone who's powerful and experienced. Being clear about your objectives will ensure that the relationship is productive and help you avoid feeling any awkwardness about needing to ignore some advice or utilize it in a different way.

MENTOR OR COACH?

A coach will provide a structured process for achieving your goals and walk you through an experience. Coaching is a paid service. With a mentor, you need to be ready to help craft the structure that will get the results you are looking for. Mentoring is often done on a volunteer basis.

The Difference between Advice and Support

I have found that advice is often based on sharing information or a strategy that has worked for the person that is giving it or is based on something they've read or seen work for others. But more often than not, advice that worked for someone else's career may not work for yours. In order for the same strategy to work for you and yield the same results, you would have to be similar people, with a similar Zone of Genius, similar personality, and a similar career vision. In my experience, this synchrony is rare.

A good mentor is probably going to give advice, while a great mentor will be more like a coach and offer support: they will take the time to learn who you are and provide thoughtful guidance and action items based on the unique circumstances of your life and career. The problem is that most people in leadership positions who serve as mentors don't really have the time, energy, or expertise to provide this kind of support. So instead, they offer generic advice, which can go something like this: "Hey, this is what I did. It worked. You should do this too."

In many ways, asking for career advice is like asking to be set up for a date. Well-intentioned friends come across two single people and think, *They're single, you're single, you should connect.* The problem is that they are only taking one shared aspect—your single status—under consideration. Similarly, you may find that someone offering well-meaning career advice may not be able to look beyond obvious circumstances to the nuances of your particular situation. Unfortunately, the advice or path that worked for one person in one industry, company, or job title may not work for another. The truth is, there are no absolute truths, essential moves, or defined paths when it comes to crafting a career.

Declining to act on advice given to you can be really difficult, especially if you admire the person providing it. When someone you respect says that you should do something, it's easy to think that you must follow their guidance or risk offending her. Make sure that you examine the advice through the lens of your Zone of Genius. If the advice doesn't feel right, discard it—even if it's coming from Oprah herself!

I have taken advice that didn't feel exciting to me but that I felt compelled to follow because someone successful suggested it. But once I started using my genius and my purpose to make decisions, the choices I needed to make that would put me on my unique path became obvious; I didn't need anyone's advice to make them. For example, it's often considered a good practice to partner with other individuals in order to build your business more quickly. But over the years I have learned that finding a partner who complements my genius and my working style is rare. I like to move quickly, and I am committed to a high level of efficiency; that working style isn't ideal for everyone. Having to work with someone else to make decisions before taking action seems inefficient, and just the thought of it is frustrating to me. Therefore, I almost always say no to anyone who suggests partnering, believing that, for me, it is bad advice.

I do, however, have one partnership with the software company BetterWorks in which our contributions are both equally valuable and complementary. BetterWorks is an enterprise software company that specializes in creating products that support performance management. The company excels in taking performance-related concepts—such as goal setting, initiating conversations, frequent feedback, and performance pulsing—and creating robust enterprise software solutions that can make these actions easy, agile, and scalable across any size organization. When the company approached me to form a partnership, I was intrigued. In our arrangement, I offer expert support to its product team on its performance-related products, and I chair its HR Advisory Council. It's a great partnership because we both are bringing our geniuses to the table. Best of all, we share a similar working style of being fast-paced and efficient. Because I evaluated the potential of the partnership to ensure it would be beneficial, I was able to confidently make one exception to my general aversion to partnerships. Although I have said no to dozens of others, many of which were recommended to me by people I know and respect, this one has been hugely beneficial for my career.

Advice Is Nice, but Support Is Necessary

I believe that asking for advice is nice, but what you really want to ask for is support. Having someone's support still allows you to make your own decision instead of that person handing the answer to you. A supportive person will never tell you what to do or say things like "If you want to do X, then you need to do Y." A coach, a therapist, or career expert can be a great source of support, as they will take the time to understand who you are and use that information to help you through the process of making the right decision.

Support can come from your mentor, from family members, or from friends who are tackling challenges that are similar to yours. I'll never forget the support I got from my friends Dana and Carol when I started my business. These women were also founding their own small businesses, and we met for coffee each week to discuss the challenges and opportunities we were facing. I wasn't looking to them for advice, and we were all clear that we needed each other to act as a sounding board. Often, sharing my ideas with them and listening to their feedback was just as exciting as the process of building my business. As a result of this special relationship, we have remained friends.

Support should ideally come from someone who:

- Takes the time to understand who you are, what your Zone of Genius is, and what is important to you.
- Doesn't give you a formula to follow.
- Listens to you more than talks to you.
- Encourages you to follow your instincts.
- Won't take it personally if you don't do what they suggest. In fact, they will encourage you to take what you want from their suggestions and ignore what isn't a good fit.
- Is forward-thinking and aware of the ever-evolving business world, so they realize that what worked ten, even five, years ago might no longer be the case.
- Is not tied to a one-size-fits-all approach.

RED FLAGS WHEN ASKING FOR ADVICE OR ACCEPTING SUPPORT

1. If the advice is overly negative, such as "Hardly anyone is successful at what you're trying to do," "The competition is really high," or "I would stay clear," disregard it. Most big ideas emerge from competitive environments. You must

remember that if a challenge is right for you, you *will* be the best at it.

2. If a person assumes that since a certain process was successful for them, that same process is the only one to follow. Proceed with caution if someone thinks of themselves as a career expert but has never made your area of focus a priority for themselves. While their suggestions may be of value, remember, it's what worked for *them*. You need to make sure it feels right to *you* before taking it on.

Filter Advice and Support through Your Zone of Genius

The best way to filter advice is to see it through the lens of your genius and your purpose. These questions can help you easily see when something directly contradicts who you are. When it's clear that's the case, you know not to follow the advice. Ask yourself the following questions that point to your genius:

- Does this advice feel right to me?
- Does the idea of this advice excite or challenge me enough to want to take it on?
- Does this advice allow me to use my genius?

These questions point toward purpose:

- Does this advice allow me to have the impact that is aligned with my purpose?
- Does this idea contradict my purpose?

Take Your Family's Advice with Caution

Take career advice with a grain of salt. Everyone thinks they're a career expert, and this might be particularly true when it comes to your parents or other family members invested in your career growth. They often operate under the assumption that if what they did worked, that's what their kids should do too. The problem with this thinking is that parents can have a hard time being completely objective about their children because they care for and love them so much. Secondly, there are real generational differences between children and parents, and the business world continues to change. Unless the parent is still actively plugged into what's going on in the workforce, he or she is likely not up to speed on the realities of the job market or his or her child's challenges and opportunities.

My brother once told me that I couldn't start my own business without getting an MBA. While getting an MBA is a great idea for some people, it was not the right move for me. Nothing excited me about the thought of getting an MBA. It seemed extremely laborious, and frankly the idea alone exhausted me. I also had many entrepreneur friends who didn't get MBAs, so I knew it wasn't essential. Yet my brother was insistent, and for a while I believed that without an MBA, I didn't have the credentials to start a business. In the end, I went with my instinct to continue on without that degree, and I'm so glad I did. I was more excited about building my business and creating my own methodology for performance, and I wanted to get started right away. I knew I had enough experience in the corporate world to learn the mechanics of running a business on my own, and I decided to follow my gut and skip the seemingly "essential" step of going to school for a degree that didn't excite me.

I did come up with a plan that allowed me to dive into my business-building venture without hesitation while staying fiscally responsible. Instead of taking my brother's advice, I decided to use some savings I was fortunate enough to have to cover my lack of income while I started my own business. If I spent more than what an MBA would cost and my business was not generating income on its own by then, I would jump ship and get a job. I am happy to report that never happened.

"Get Good Grades, Go to College, Get a Job" Doesn't Work for Everyone

Our penchant for relying on other people's advice didn't just start in the workplace: it's likely that you can trace your experience back to high school when you decided to go or not go to college. It may have been the first time in your life that you heard a message and took it as dogma. Let's unpack this one piece of advice, consider the source, and see if it worked for you and your genius.

The traditional message surrounding college used to be that if you want to be professionally successful, you need at least a bachelor's degree. While it's true that there are companies that won't hire new employees unless they have a college degree, today, more are looking at the applicant's entire experience. If your goal is to be a lawyer or a doctor or anyone in the professional services, you have to get a college degree. If you want to work for a major company and work your way up to be a manager, you probably need a college degree. But if you want to take the world by storm, start your own company, develop software, or freelance in the gig economy, you don't necessarily need a four-year commitment and the boatload of debt that often comes with it.

But here's the rub: some people who don't go to college think they're not good enough to get the kind of job they want. They feel embarrassed about their lack of higher education or feel unworthy of a prestigious career path. Luckily, this attitude is slowly changing with increased accessibility to information: if people want to learn a particular skill, they can find the tools they need online or from sources other than traditional education programs.

If you didn't go to college, don't despair: some of the most successful people either left college early or skipped the college experience entirely. According to *Time* magazine, Mark Zuckerberg, Steve Jobs, Bill Gates, filmmaker James Cameron, Tom Hanks, Harrison Ford, and Lady Gaga all dropped out of college to pursue their dreams.[27] In their cases, the university setting was actually a barrier to reaching their goals. By striking out on their own and pursuing their goals directly, they were able to achieve great things.

If going to college was the right decision for you, you may have felt intense pressure to get into a "good" school—maybe even one in the Ivy League. The association between an Ivy League education and intelligence has become so strong in our culture, it's no wonder that many people believe that the only way to become successful is to graduate from a name brand school. I know when I was growing up, I thought, *If I get into an Ivy League school, my future success is a guarantee.* When I didn't get accepted to my first-choice schools, I assumed that I would have a harder time finding success than others who had access to that kind of education.

The reality is that no school, no matter how prestigious, can guarantee success for all of its students. After all, as we've discussed, success looks different to every person! If you didn't go to an Ivy League school, you can stop beating yourself up about it. And if you are contemplating graduate school, your choice in school should be driven by finding the best fit for your goals, not by the school's name.

Research has shown that there can actually be disadvantages to attending an elite school. According to William Deresiewicz, author of the book *Excellent Sheep: The Miseducation of the American Elite and the Way to a Meaningful Life*, having an "elite" education trains you in a particular way of speaking, which makes it difficult to talk to people who aren't like you. William spent fourteen years in higher education and has a handful of Ivy League degrees. He writes, "Elite schools pride themselves on their diversity, but that diversity is almost entirely a matter of ethnicity and race. With respect to class, these schools are largely—indeed, increasingly—homogeneous." Deresiewicz makes an important point here. Those who attend Ivy League schools may have fewer opportunities to experience diversity and collaborate with people who come from a wide variety of backgrounds, potentially putting them at a disadvantage later in their careers.

Additionally, elite education often trains you to follow rules rather than the desire to follow your own path. To get into an elite school, you must jump through all the right hoops in all the right ways, from scoring well on the SATs, to getting the right internships, to saying the right things in interviews. Society is inundated with tips and tricks on navigating this path to school acceptance, and there is a booming industry of tutors, consultants, and coaches all geared toward helping you make it to the top. This entire process of gaining acceptance to elite schools primes us with the idea that there is only one right way of doing things. And it only gets worse once we get to college, where we are absorbed into the competition for the same internships and coveted jobs. This type of thinking keeps us from pursuing work we love. When you refuse to prioritize joy and fulfillment in your work, your performance suffers. In the race to the top, you might actually get stuck in mediocrity.

Lastly, an elite education promotes a fixed mind-set. Elite education pushes us to believe that where we fall on the scale of standardized tests and college rankings automatically determines our worth and the level of success that we should aspire to. But this is not true! Having this fixed mind-set is actually one of the worst things we can do for our performance and impact in life. In her research, Stanford University psychologist Carol Dweck discovered than an essential quality of success is the growth mind-set—the belief that you can always improve and that success is linked more strongly to effort than more fixed factors such as intelligence.

The truth is, there is no longer a one-size-fits-all approach to success. The key is to understand who you are and recognize that there are endless ways to be successful in life. Your task is to find the solutions, the environments, the companies, and the places that are right for you. When you stop listening to the advice of others and do what's right for you, that's when you are going to use your genius to maximize your potential. Realize that you have so much more to give than what you accomplished, or didn't, in college. So give yourself a break when it comes to assessing your value and your potential for success. Know yourself, and value your genius.

Feedback Is Never Bad

Many people have a love–hate relationship with feedback. We love hearing positive feedback, and we fear feedback that is negative. The fear of negative feedback is caused by the belief that if someone says you're not doing a good job, you aren't good enough, or by the fear that we have to be someone else in order to succeed. What's crazy about this is that we fear changing jobs so much that most people will stay in the wrong job, continue to fear the negative feedback that validates the poor fit, and embrace the drudgery that is involved with trying to be someone they're not.

This is why understanding how to manage positive and negative feedback is just as important as seeking it. It's a mirror to how others are perceiving you and your behavior. There are many times when we're working hard but we may be oblivious to how we are coming across to others. In this situation, feedback is your friend. It can help validate whether you're having the impact that is aligned with your purpose and let you know when you're not using your genius (e.g., you may not be performing because you're bored or overwhelmed). If you can separate yourself emotionally from the negative feedback and see it as an opportunity, you can use it to your benefit. It can help validate the work you're doing in building the Genius Habit.

Feedback also needs to be filtered the same way that advice does. Consider the source. Who is delivering it? Is it true for you? If not, where is the disconnect coming from? What can you learn from it? What is this feedback telling you about your situation?

Matthew Turns Negative Feedback into Positive Change

Matthew had just taken a new job as a senior executive at a large organization when we started working together. He was managing a department of about two hundred people, and I suggested he get some feedback on his performance from his peers and his manager ninety days into his new position.

He received both positive and negative feedback, but it was the negative comments that proved to be the most useful. One person on his team called him arrogant. I found that feedback shocking because Matthew was one of the least arrogant people I have met. We couldn't disregard the feedback, but we could dissect it to find out how best to use the data.

Instead of becoming defensive, Matthew decided to view the feedback as a glimpse into the company's culture. We realized that although Matthew wasn't arrogant, he was being perceived as such because deep down he believed that his company's culture was flawed, that it was old school and not forward-thinking. His internal thoughts were displayed via his nonverbal behavior, and that behavior was being translated as arrogance by a few key senior people.

Once we understood the disconnect, we worked together to change his mind-set. The good news was that Matthew's job did require him to use his genius, and he was having the impact that was meaningful to him; the negative feedback helped us see a blind spot. I was able to show him that rather than getting defensive, he could look at the feedback for what it was—data. I suggested that he buy into the current culture and really practice believing in it. It was the only way to change his nonverbal communication. We decided that even though the company culture was not the perfect fit, trying to work with it was the best strategy for him. Within a few weeks of doing this, Matthew started getting positive feedback from his peers: they saw a difference.

Develop a Feedback Loop

If you're at a company that doesn't have a formal performance review process or way of providing regular feedback, I would encourage you to make soliciting feedback a priority. It's always a good idea to be aware of your impact and take the pulse of your work situation. Use the following four questions, which are similar to the questions you used earlier in the book to identify your genius, to gauge your current impact and performance. These questions are a way to uncover any performance issues that others see that you may not. They're also a way to understand how clearly your colleagues see you for who you are. You can use them to gauge whether others are witnessing you operating in your Zone of Genius. To start, send these questions to a select group of people who work closely with you and know you well. Have them send their answers back to you.

1. What have you valued most about my recent performance?
2. How would you describe my unique approach to my role? Am I consistently bringing this unique perspective to my team and my job?

3. How has working with me impacted your work experience or business results recently? What has been the biggest change?

4. What, if any, constructive feedback do you have for me regarding my performance, management, or leadership style?

Honor Your Intuition

Intuition comes from an amalgamation of what you've learned throughout your life. According to occupational psychologist Gerard Hodgkinson, intuition is the result of the way our brains store, process, and retrieve information.[28] The brain is drawing on past experiences and external cues to make an instantaneous decision, leaving us with a general feeling that something is right or wrong. Psychologist Gerd Gigerenzer has spent his career focusing on the ways in which we use intuition to make the right decisions. In his view, gut feelings are tools we have for an uncertain world, and they are based on our experience, which he considers to be an unconscious form of intelligence. In a 2014 interview with the *Harvard Business Review*, Gigerenzer stated, "I've worked with large companies and asked decision makers how often they base an important professional decision on that gut feeling. In the companies I've worked with, which are large international companies, about 50 percent of all decisions are at the end a gut decision."[29]

Clearly, intuition is a source of wisdom that you should use in your life at work. Paying more attention to your intuition and honoring it is all about building your awareness of yourself. By trusting your instinct, you're making use of your own wisdom.

I believe that great decisions come from a combination of instinct and data, and you can use your Zone of Genius as your personal data. As I mentioned earlier, when you make career decisions keeping in mind your genius and your purpose, you can more easily see if a job is a match for who you are and what fulfills you. Your instinct is usually right, but your rational mind craves external validation. Your excitement, or lack of it, in response to this decision is your intuition speaking to you. If you feel good about it, and the decision also allows you to use your genius and have the impact of your purpose, you're golden.

It's also important to know when to honor your instinct when you feel that you don't have the experience to move forward. That's when it's great to seek out support or advice, keeping in mind the guidelines we've discussed in this chapter.

Get External Support or Turn Inward?

Here are some questions to help you navigate this decision point the next time you are faced with the question of going with your instinct versus getting outside help. Answer yes or no to the following questions:

1. Are you in need of help with a problem or solution that has never been solved before?

   YES
   NO

2. Is the underlying problem a lack of confidence? Do you have ideas of how to tackle the challenge, but don't believe you can accomplish what you're imagining?

   YES
   NO

3. Do you devalue the knowledge you have and find yourself consistently seeking outside sources in the form of classes and degrees?

   YES
   NO

4. Do you lack expertise? Have you accumulated less than one thousand hours of experience in a particular field?

   YES
   NO

5. Do you have *Imposter Syndrome* (meaning you consistently feel that you are a fraud) when it comes to creating something that is new and is a complete extension of your ideas?

   YES
   NO

0–2 Yeses:

It seems that you may benefit from some support. You're confident, but you may not have the experience needed to rely on your own intuition. Usually in the early days of building expertise, having support—someone to help you think through ideas or provide suggestions that are tactical—can be helpful. Just remember that if someone is making suggestions that don't feel right or aren't aligned with who you are, discard them and seek support from others.

3 Yeses:

You are having some confidence issues, but what's really holding you back has more to do with tactical steps than with creating a new path. In this situation, reach out to someone for advice or support but make sure you take what that person says with a grain of salt. If what that person suggests doesn't resonate, don't use it. At the same time, tap into your own wisdom and expertise.

4–5 Yeses:

Your real issue is that you don't believe you are good enough to trust your instincts. You have ideas, you may have experience, but you don't value them as much as someone who either has a degree or someone who has been doing what you're doing for longer. However, before you reach out and ask for help or advice, wait. Tap into your own wisdom, believe in your unique perspective, and take a risk. That is how innovation happens.

Jeff Bezos Honored His Intuition

Jeff Bezos studied computer science and electrical engineering at Princeton University and after graduation went to work on Wall Street. In 1990, he became the youngest senior vice president at the investment firm D. E. Shaw. Four years later he came up with the idea for Amazon.com. He envisioned a bookstore without a store and wanted to become an internet merchant of books.

Bezos really admired his boss and asked for his advice regarding his idea of quitting his high-paying job to start this venture. His boss replied, "That's a great idea for someone who doesn't have a job. You already have a great job." His boss's advice wasn't mean-spirited, but it definitely wasn't supportive. This advice gave Bezos pause. In fact, he says it made him rethink starting Amazon. Feeling torn, Bezos consulted with his wife, who suggested that he give it a try; he could always go back to banking if it didn't work out. He agreed, moved his family from New York City to Seattle, started Amazon.com from his garage, and the rest is history. When he tells the story, he says that there was something inside him that couldn't put the idea to rest; he felt he had to give it a try.

Jeff Bezos followed his intuition and didn't look back. He took a major, high stakes risk; he went for it. Amazon is currently the world's largest internet sales company.[30]

When you can honor your intuition, take feedback from other people as data, and find the right support, you're building the habit of becoming more self-aware. This deepening commitment to yourself is the way to find true joy at work because you are leveraging yourself in everything you do. When you can trust yourself and begin to use external resources as tools rather than crutches, you will be better equipped to fully maximize your potential, rather than feeling like you're on someone else's treadmill going nowhere.

The Next Step

The next chapter is about mindfulness, the ability to stay in the present. You'll learn that mindfulness is a powerful tool for building awareness, lowering stress, and staying true to your Zone of Genius.

PART IV

MINDFULNESS

CHAPTER 8

YOUR SELF-WORTH IS ABOUT CONFIDENCE, NOT PRAISE

Question: How confident are you?

Genius Action Plan: Get Your Performance
Data from the Source—*You*

If your Zone of Genius is the perfect combination of the type of thinking and problem-solving you most enjoy, applied to the type of work that matches your purpose, it makes sense that the more you know about yourself, the more easily you can create a positive working experience that is easy to replicate. Identifying your genius and your purpose is the first step to operating in your Zone of Genius; the next is understanding and owning their value. That's where confidence comes from.

Confidence isn't about someone else giving you a pat on the

back for doing a great job: it's the feeling that comes from within you when you appreciate and value yourself no matter what. It comes from understanding who you are and knowing the contribution you can make.

When I was at Capital One as part of the analyst team, my confidence was low because I was trying to be someone who I was not by working in a very analytical job. Now, because I know my genius and my purpose, I feel confident even when I'm surrounded by lots of highly analytical people. I know that particular skill set is not what I'm best at, and I also know that's OK. I can appreciate that skill set in others because rather than trying to be like them, I can embrace their strengths wholeheartedly and, at the same time, know that I bring something of equal value to the table. This understanding builds confidence because I can appreciate and value who I am no matter who I'm around and no matter what environment I am in.

Confidence is a trait that everyone wants to have because it is thought to lead to great success, yet it is an aspect of ourselves that is often neglected or not fully analyzed. Even though we know the importance of it, the act of building it is somewhat still mysterious. More often than not, we notice our lack of confidence before we notice an abundance of it. Think of this book as the first of many stepping-stones to building your confidence muscle. The result is that you'll be less afraid of failure and you won't have to think you need to be perfect in order to succeed. The truth is, once you begin to use your genius, you'll confidently recognize that you already have the key building blocks you need to succeed.

Remember that you have the power to control your thoughts and the way they influence your actions. You'll deepen your self-awareness and find what makes you feel most confident. Then, you can call on that feeling anytime. Without getting too woo-woo, I'll show you how quieting the negative noise inside your head increases your confidence. The key is practicing mindfulness, the ability to be completely in the present moment so that you can understand your reactions to triggers and gain more conscious-ness about these reactions. When you can act intentionally instead of instinctually, you will immediately see a surge in confidence because you are not at the mercy of your subconscious behavior.

Strong emotional reactions are often accompanied by nega-tive mental chatter, yet few of us are aware of its power over our thinking and behavior—and our career potential. The negativity that plays inside our heads—and trust me, we all hear something like *I'm not good enough, smart enough, savvy enough*—clouds our thinking and limits what we see as possible. Ultimately, it affects our work by affecting our perspective of our value. In short, neg-ative internal chatter affects your confidence. Add a lack of con-fidence to poor health habits, such as not getting enough sleep or not exercising, and the negative mental chatter is even less controllable. If you're not prepared to be at your best in terms of physical stamina, you can't manage your negative mental energy.

How Triggers Affect Your Confidence

Confidence shouldn't be fleeting: we should feel good most of the time about who we are and how we work. But sadly, this is not the case for most. We all have baggage from our past that has created negative emotions and thoughts, which show up when we bump against a specific related trigger. Have you ever noticed how some things really aggravate you, but you're not sure why? Or you've had a reaction to an event everyone else around seems to be OK with?

Everyone experiences these triggers, and it's in these moments that you aren't being the best version of yourself. Most people aren't aware that they're triggered until they've done something that they wish they hadn't, like yell and scream at an employee, slam their hands on their desk, or otherwise act irrationally. In other situations, it's not as noticeable to others: a triggering event can increase your negative mental chatter, which can lead to a panic attack, high anxiety, or extreme worry, and then you're not able to operate well at work. The problem is twofold: first, the trigger sends you off on a direction you wish you hadn't gone, and second, it's hard to reverse the damage you've caused if your behavior was affected by a trigger.

Most people have a handful of triggers. I know that I have about six, a couple being lack of responsibility and lack of responsiveness. Just like getting triggered when I'm not seen, when I perceive that someone hasn't acted responsibly or when someone doesn't respond to me within a certain time frame, I have a charged reaction that's exaggerated. Lack of responsiveness is connected to not being seen, because when someone doesn't respond, I instantly feel as though that person didn't see me, and I feel rejected.

Once you understand your core emotional challenge, you will notice that many of your triggers are different yet similar versions of your core emotional challenge, just as these additional triggers are very close to my core emotional challenge of not being seen. Any of them could certainly undermine your confidence. If you can slow down and be observant, you can more easily see what your triggers are. There's a lot of power that you can reclaim by being aware of when you're triggered, what's causing that trigger, naming it, and then being able to manage yourself through the moment more effectively. This process is another example of mindfulness. Once you can identify your triggers, you'll be better prepared to deal with them the next time they show up. You can react from a more rational space, which allows you to slow down and create behavior that's more aligned with who you want to be.

Abby Hates Being Unprepared

My client Abby gets triggered whenever she feels that she is unprepared. She is a perfectionist, so her version of preparing for a meeting meant spending hours reading reports and understanding the current market conditions. If she ever walked into a meeting and hadn't thought through every possible outcome, she would become anxious, get really down on herself, and lose confidence. If someone asked her a question she wasn't prepared for, she would walk out of the meeting and chastise herself for hours, battling the negative chatter rather than doing productive work.

I told Abby that the first step to undoing this connection in her brain between the unpreparedness trigger and the outcome was to identify what was setting her off. I helped her realize that something about being unprepared was a trigger from her past, and she was able to connect it to the fact that her father was constantly telling her that she wasn't good enough. In order to gain her father's praise, she felt that she always had to avoid any instance of failure. Most of her negative mental chatter surrounded this feeling that no matter what she did, she just wasn't good enough.

Once Abby was able to identify her triggers, we began to work on rewiring the negative thought process into a more positive one. Together we created another message that she could use when those negative thoughts came up. She got into the habit of saying, "I am as prepared as I can be, and lack of preparation is not a reflection of my value" whenever she felt anxious in a meeting. Just making that one change started to reduce the impact of her negative chatter.

Since then, she has told me that the more she practices

overriding her negative chatter with positive thoughts, such as during those moments when she's not completely prepared for a meeting, she can guard against the emotional trigger and pro-actively bolster her confidence. Abby said, "Now that I am clear about what in the present triggers me, I can see that it comes from my past. I can now be calm and contribute the best that I can in the moment. I realize I have the power to shift this internal messaging."

Genius Action Plan: Get Your Performance Data from the Source—*You*

This exercise will help you pinpoint reasons you are feeling anxious, stressed, or not confident at work. Spend a couple of weeks observing and being present in the moments when you're experiencing stress, anxiety, or a lack of confidence. Look carefully at incidents at work and at home. Make a list of these moments and ask yourself the following questions. Pay attention to what triggered these moments and then what the negative chatter is in your head that caused your reaction.

Ask yourself:

• What about this incident is similar to a negative event I may have experienced in the past?
• What caused it?

- Is this incident related to my core emotional challenge?
- If it's not, what other childhood event in my past may be the trigger for this reaction?

Once you're able to figure out where the negative messages are coming from, you can rewire your brain to your advantage by creating positive messages or mantras that are in opposition to the negative messaging. By rewriting those messages, you can control your mental state. In addition, slowing down and practicing being more present and aware of the moments when you're triggered, you can begin to understand them more and as a result understand yourself. This is the essence of the practice of mindfulness. You're able to recognize and ignore negative internal messages instead of being derailed by them. Undoing these negative talk patterns is a powerful behavior change that will immediately boost your confidence.

AVOID BLAMING OTHERS AND JUMPING TO THE WRONG CONCLUSIONS

How many times have you had the feeling that something is "off" at work? It could be as simple as having a bad conversation with your manager. In these moments it's easy to immediately pinpoint an external cause instead of identifying the root cause (which may, in fact, be you). However, these are the exact moments that indicate that you are being triggered. It's also a great time to use the Performance Tracker. The feeling that something is off is a bread crumb to your psyche, which is why it's important to reflect on this feeling before jumping to conclusions about your performance or your relationship with your manager.

The Confidence Game: Men versus Women

There is a real difference between the way men and women associate with confidence. According to a 2014 article published in *The Atlantic* titled "The Confidence Gap," evidence shows that women are less self-assured than men, resulting in the continued practice of men being promoted faster and paid more, despite the fact that there are more women in the workplace. In this article, the continued failure to break through the glass ceiling is viewed through the lens of women's "acute lack of confidence." Katty Kay and Claire Shipman, who authored the article, in addition to the book *The Confidence Code,* write:

As we talked with women, dozens of them, all accomplished and credentialed, we kept bumping up against a dark spot that we couldn't quite identify, a force clearly holding them back. Why did the successful investment banker mention to us that she didn't really deserve the big promotion she'd just got? What did it mean when the engineer who'd been a pioneer in her industry for decades told us offhandedly that she wasn't sure she was really the best choice to run her firm's new big project? Our experience suggests that the power centers of this nation are zones of female self-doubt—that is, when they include women at all… Compared with men, women don't consider themselves as ready for promotions, they predict they'll do worse on tests, and they generally underestimate their abilities.[31]

The research they cite is eye-opening. Linda Babcock, a professor of economics at Carnegie Mellon University, found that men initiate salary negotiations four times as often as women do, and that when women do negotiate, their lack of confidence leads them to ask for 30 percent less than a man in a similar situation would.[32] In comparison, men err on the side of *honest overconfidence*, a term coined by Ernesto Reuben at Columbia Business School to describe men's inherent and consistent ability to inflate their success. Reuben says, "They [men] honestly believe their performance is 30 per cent better than it really is. Women, on the other hand, consistently rated their past performance only about 15 percent higher than it actually was."

The bottom line is that men and women have shown marked differences in their beliefs in their capabilities. This research blew my mind because, as a woman, it was hard to swallow that this phenomenon was real and that most women weren't aware of the difference. This is one area where women can look to men for inspiration. There are a lot of things in the world that we can't control, but we can control how we feel about ourselves and our abilities. My wish is that women can learn to own this difference and do the work to eliminate their lack of confidence.

Imposter Syndrome: We Don't Believe We're the Real Deal

Imposter Syndrome is rampant in both men and women through-out the workforce. It's the feeling that you don't have the abilities other people think you have and that you are likely to fail. Sheryl Sandberg talks about this phenomenon in her book *Lean In*, when she describes often feeling unqualified for the executive positions she held at Google and Facebook. If Sheryl Sandberg feels like an imposter, you can bet we all do.

Understanding your Zone of Genius can help you conquer Imposter Syndrome. First, recognize that getting ahead requires you to learn on the job, and does not mean you have to know the right answers all of the time. Operating in your Zone of Genius can help you recognize the thinking and impact that you can contribute to solve problems. It will also help you see when your genius isn't the skill set necessary to get the job done, so that you can find others who have the genius for the task and collaborate with them.

Believing in yourself and having the confidence to dive into problems that you're ready to solve is a behavior you want to practice. In fact, taking risks and not being afraid of the unknown is more important than actually being an expert. The idea that real leaders know everything is well on its way out. There is so much readily available information for anyone to access; the process of problem-solving is now more important than the facts themselves.

You may also have a trigger that is similar to Imposter Syndrome if being a fraud is connected to your core emotional challenge. The fix? The same as building your confidence: increase your awareness. Being more aware of having this feeling is the first step. Do you know the precise moment when it comes up? Is it a constant feeling? Is it only when you're in a specific situation, such as a board meeting, a team meeting, or when you're making a presentation? Or is it when you're responsible for a deadline or doing analysis? If you can track these situations, you will know where and how you get tripped up, and then can begin the work of rewiring your confidence. And remember, those that come across as being super confident are just working harder behind the scenes to rewire their thinking. Overcoming Imposter Syndrome requires effort.

The Elon Musk Story:
Making Failure Part of Your Success

The ultimate goal for building your confidence muscle is to maintain confidence regardless of what is happening in the external world. Setbacks and failures are part of life, but you can't let them destroy you. Having true confidence means that no matter what happens, you know yourself, you believe in yourself, and you can face failure with resiliency.

Take Elon Musk, a man known for his billion-dollar ventures, as a perfect example. The founder of SpaceX didn't have a linear path to success. In fact, he had some epic missteps along the way. But Musk didn't let failed rocket launches and the brink of bankruptcy scare him away from his goals. His failures can be read like a resume:

1995: Unsuccessfully applied for a job at Netscape (although a big deal at the time, where is Netscape today?)

1996: Ousted as CEO of his own company, Zip2, a company that licensed online city guide software to newspapers

2000: Ousted from PayPal while on his honeymoon

2001–2002: Attempted to buy rockets from Russia to start SpaceX but no deal to be had

2006: First SpaceX rocket launch ends in an explosion

2008: Both Tesla and SpaceX on the brink of bankruptcy

2013–2015: More rocket explosions

2014: Tesla Model S has problems with spontaneous combustion of batteries

2018: Elon Musk's business is less than perfect, but he's worth $14.8 billion

Musk has clearly had epic failures that at times have kept him from moving forward. Yet he never gave up and has learned from every one of them.[33] He says, "Failure is an option here. If things are not failing, you are not innovating enough." Also, "I think it is possible for ordinary people to choose to be extraordinary." I agree.

Adopting a Growth Mind-Set

Your mind-set is something that you're completely in control of. Your mind-set is how you structure your thoughts and how you operate within the world. It's also how you manage your mind and your mental chatter. The power comes when you can manage your mind-set and create habits that allow you to build confidence and have more peace and joy at work and in your life.

In her groundbreaking book, *Mindset,* Carol Dweck, a social and developmental psychologist at Stanford University, describes two mind-sets in opposition. A fixed mind-set does not allow people the luxury of changing: they already are who they are.

However, a growth mind-set allows people to rise to a challenge, to change and grow. She writes that intelligence can be enhanced if you believe that you can change it. Dweck writes, "When you enter a mind-set, you enter a new world. In one world—the world of fixed traits—success is about proving you're smart or talented. Validating yourself. In the other—the world of changing qualities—it's about stretching yourself to learn something new. Developing yourself."

Dweck noted that students with a fixed mind-set had higher levels of depression and were more likely to ruminate over their problems and setbacks, tormenting themselves with the idea that the setbacks meant they were incompetent or unworthy. Their failures labeled them and left them no route to success. However, a growth mind-set encourages you to put a positive spin on failures and, like Elon Musk, learn from them.

When I was in school, I was always a good student, but when I would get a bad grade I would feel like a failure and worry that I wasn't good enough. I definitely had a fixed mind-set. It was no wonder, because our education system is set up to promote a fixed mind-set. *You're either an A student or you're not. You're either talented or you're not.* It wasn't until I started my own business and discovered my Zone of Genius that I started to see failures as opportunities. I now welcome failures and instead of overreacting negatively, think about other factors, such as, *What can I do better next time? What role will hard work, my genius, and focus play?* When

I took those into consideration, I was able to move into a growth mind-set—and you can, too.

> ## A GROWTH MIND-SET + ZONE OF GENIUS = CONFIDENCE
>
> When you can believe in yourself despite any setback and acknowledge that there are aspects of your work that don't align with your strengths without losing confidence in your skills, you've combined a growth mind-set with your Zone of Genius. When you're able to own who you are and own who you're not, I believe that's true confidence.

Shutting Down the "I'm Not Smart Enough" Conversation

It's really easy to feel like you're not smart enough, especially if you were ever labeled as less intelligent than others in school or early in life. Being told you don't have the same intellectual capacity as others around you obviously affects your self-image and can become something of a self-fulfilling prophecy. But interestingly, the same damage can occur if you have been praised for being naturally smart.

You would think being called smart would help you perform

better, but Carol Dweck proved otherwise. She developed a simple experiment in which she showed that both criticism and praise can undermine our ability to cope with challenges. Dweck asked young children to solve a simple puzzle. Most did so with little difficulty. But then she told some, but not all, how very bright and capable they were. The children who were not told they were smart were more motivated to tackle increasingly difficult puzzles and exhibited higher levels of confidence.[34] The idea that praise can cause a lack of confidence may seem counterintuitive, yet Dweck's research proves the point. While you might think that everyone would enjoy being called smart, it turns out that it doesn't necessarily help them. It ultimately inhibits confidence, because when you're told you're smart, you may see failure as a sign that you may not be as smart as you've been told.

As you progress in your career, you may be labeled based on your skills. Although managers are quick to sort employees into categories based on how they're performing, calling people *smart* or *not smart* isn't useful. It's also probably inaccurate. According to psychologist Howard Gardner, there are nine types of intelligence. The fact that there are so many ways to measure intelligence is why it's nearly impossible to know if someone is "smart" or not. Clearly, labeling people as *smart* or *slow* or something else isn't taking the full scope of their intelligence into consideration. Worse, the one making the label has no real way of assessing someone accurately. They're just making an assumption based on what they have observed; their perception could be different from others because of their own biases and definition of intelligence.

Everyone thinks they can assess others' intelligence, yet no one is truly capable of doing so—unless you are an expert performing an evaluation. But more importantly, no one at your place of work has the authority to decide who is smart and who is not. Instead of defaulting to describing someone as smart or not smart, be more mindful: try slowing down and speak in more detail about what you're observing. If you see two people working well together, tell them they are great collaborators. Pay more attention to and honor them for what they're actually bringing to the table versus generalizing with a label that isn't that helpful. Providing more detailed and precise positive feedback goes a long way to bolster another person's confidence.

If you want to feel intellectually confident, actively find ways to operate more often in your Zone of Genius. Ever since I started developing my Genius Habit, I have found ways to use my Zone of Genius at work, and I've become more confident. I don't pay attention to labels that could define me or my intelligence because I'm clear about my strengths and weaknesses, and I try to align my work with my strengths. I'm also attuned to the fact that I have the ability to learn, grow, and attain new skills that are needed to keep stretching my expertise. This doesn't mean that my Zone of Genius will change over time. What will change is how I apply it and my depth of expertise. As I become more adept at using it, I have observed my expertise deepening, which encourages me to challenge my genius further with more complex and more rewarding challenges.

Steve Overcame Doubt with Growth Mind-Set

My client Steve came to me because he was struggling with confidence. Steve was a consultant for a large firm. He liked his job but dreamed of starting his own consulting practice. He wanted to make the shift from doing the client work himself to managing a team of consultants who worked directly for him. He also felt stagnant in the typical consulting culture and wanted to create a new and more vibrant workplace. Yet he was stuck in the idea stage because he had so much self-doubt. He was plagued with Imposter Syndrome, which made him feel that he was never quite ready to open his own shop. He told me that he was constantly hearing a voice in his head saying, *Who am I to be a CEO? Can someone like me really accomplish this dream?*

We discovered that Steve's core emotional challenge was a result of being neglected and often ignored as a young child. His pain of being neglected made his purpose clear: he loves helping other people feel like they aren't alone, either by giving them support or mentoring them through problems. This purpose is a perfect match for consulting work, and Steve was excited to see how the choices he made fit together. His dream of starting his own business was also aligned with his genius, which we called a Creative Possibilitarian. Steve was full of ideas that would make his business different from the competition, and he had the experience to make it happen. He wanted to create a culture that allowed everyone to do the work that was aligned with their Zone of Genius, because he felt that this would be the best environment that would allow consultants to flourish. His current company had a very different culture, and most of the employees were overworked, burned out, and neglected.

My next assignment was addressing Steve's crippling self-doubt. Using the Performance Tracker we identified two major triggers as we started tracking the moments when he felt the least amount of confidence. The first trigger occurred when he felt overwhelmed with too much work. The busier he was at his day job, the less time he had for building his own business. Yet the busyness made him feel anxious and that he would never have the time or energy to devote to his own business. The second trigger occurred whenever he lost a client. When a client disappeared without an apparent reason, Steve would go into a spiral of self-doubt. These instances were not consistent enough to become performance issues, but when they happened it had a significant impact on his morale and led him to believe that he was not capable of starting his own business.

Once we identified Steve's triggers, I helped create some

new messages for him to say to himself that would address the negative chatter that created his self-doubt. The first was, "I can be a CEO and I am capable." The second message was geared toward his first trigger, as well as his ultimate goal of starting his own firm: "I can't take on work that takes me away from building my dream job." The third message was geared toward his second trigger: "When someone leaves, it rarely has to do with my capabilities, it means it wasn't a great fit."

We also started working on developing Steve's growth mindset. He filled out the Performance Tracker every week, reminding himself that he believed in his skills and reframing problems as opportunities. After a couple of months of rewiring his self-doubt Steve felt like a new person. He was finally ready to build his own business. We began to create timelines and action steps he could take to make his dream a reality. Within a year, his new business was launched, and he reported back to me that he was happier and more confident than ever.

The simple practice of reversing Steve's self-doubt allowed him to see that he could achieve beyond what he thought was possible. Steve and I are still in touch today, and every time he falls for his old triggers, I remind him that his genius and purpose are so clear that he was made to do this work; he just needs to continue to believe what was true all along.

Which Mind-Set Do You Have?

According to Carol Dweck, you live either in a fixed world where the way you are is not going to change, or you believe that you have the potential for endless personal growth. Answer these questions to see if you have a growth or fixed mind-set. Which mind-set do you agree with more? You can be a mixture, but most people lean toward one or the other:

1. Your genius is something very basic about your way of working, and you can't change it very much.

    AGREE
    DISAGREE

2. You can learn new skills, but you can't increase your intelligence.

    AGREE
    DISAGREE

3. No matter how much aptitude you have for a particular task, you can always change it quite a bit, even your intelligence.

    AGREE
    DISAGREE

4. You can always substantially deepen your genius.

    AGREE
    DISAGREE

If you agree with statements 1 and 2, you most likely have a fixed mind-set. If you agree with statements 3 and 4, you most likely have a growth mind-set.

Mantras for Building Mindfulness and Confidence

While it's important to create messages that speak to your particular triggers, many people struggle with similar issues. Many of us have the same core emotional challenges, and we all likely suffer from Imposter Syndrome at one point or another.

Here are a few mantras that I believe can help anyone. Feel free to pick and choose the ones that resonate with you.

- I can create the success I want.
- Other people's opinions of me are just their perception.
- Failures are opportunities to grow, learn, and be better.
- I respect and admire my Zone of Genius and know that I add value.
- My negative mental chatter is not real.
- Confidence is my birthright.
- When I feel like an imposter, it's a sign that I am on the right path.
- When I am using my Zone of Genius, I tap into my brilliance.
- I am capable of achieving my dream job.
- Negative feedback is just data helping me access fit with my job.

The Next Step

Mindfulness is not limited to how you think—it's also about the choices you make every day about your physical health, which directly affect your work. In the next chapter, you'll learn why maintaining high energy is a practice that affects not only the way you feel, but also the way you think.

CHAPTER 9

RAMP UP YOUR ENERGY

Question: Are you really productive?

Genius Action Plan: Switch Your Orientation from Sacrificing Your Time and Well-Being to Prioritizing Your Well-Being

B y now, you should feel confident about what your genius is. You may even be envisioning how you're going to apply it at work, how it's going to make you more efficient, more joyful, and more mindful. The truth is, the more frequently you use your genius throughout your day, the more confident you'll become, because you'll be replacing the bare bones of competency with confidence. This will free up even more mental energy so that you can take your job to the next level.

Being Excellent at Everything Is a Bad Strategy

We often view striving for excellence in all areas of our job or career as the key to getting ahead. We've been taught that more is always better, and as a result most people are on the constant quest for more: more information, more education, or more credentials. But the truth is, trying to be good at everything is a bad strategy. Trying to do everything perfectly is a huge energy drain, and the quest for perfection leads to a tendency to be overstretched. Many of my clients have shared that the way they've gotten to the top is to always overprepare. While in theory this sounds like a great strategy, being overly prepared takes a lot of time and is not particularly efficient. Excellence is an expensive skill: people exert a lot of energy trying to be an expert at everything rather than prioritizing how they can best use their genius and delegating the rest.

Those in search of excellence are willing to sacrifice their well-being, their energy, and their health to do what they think they need to do to succeed. Even worse than the toll that commitment to complete excellence takes on your body and mind, the underlying message of over-preparedness is *I'm not good enough*—a clear indicator of less-than-robust confidence. If you have an obsessive need to be an expert at everything rather than to deepen your sense of expertise and connect with your genius, you'll never be able to prioritize your work in the way that best aligns with your genius, and you'll always feel inadequate.

Focusing on the work you are best at, rather than trying to be a jack-of-all-trades, sets the stage for experiencing less stress and feeling more confident. A study supporting this notion comes from Cameron Anderson, a professor of organizational behavior at the University of California, Berkeley. He repeatedly quizzed 250 students over the course of a semester, asking the participants to see if they recognized historic names and events from a list that included some complete fabrications. He found that the students who chose the most fake names and appeared confident in their selection were regarded by their peers as the most respected and admired of the participants, even though they were often wrong. This research shows that the students who knew less but appeared to know more were the winners: when it comes to perception by others, confidence trumped competence.[35] Which isn't to say that you should throw competence out the window. But what is more important to note is that others are drawn to confidence. Trying to be someone you're not to appear more competent will backfire.

Are You Close to Burnout?

It's surprisingly easy to ignore the signs of burnout. You might be so determined to meet a deadline or achieve a goal that you miss the red flags and warning signs that something is about to go very wrong. If you're not conscious of what your body is telling you, you'll likely hit a wall before you even realize something isn't right.

How many of the following energy pitfalls can you relate to? Maybe one more than the others. Maybe you're not close to burning out, or you are already in burnout mode and don't even know it. Do any of these warning signs feel familiar?

1. You wake up in the middle of the night with your mind or heart racing.
2. You're always in reactive mode.
3. You constantly worry about the future.
4. You're often irritable or quick to anger.
5. You haven't had more than five hours of sleep a night in weeks.
6. You've forgotten what joy feels like.

The good news is that there are more productive ways of behaving in the moment so that you can avoid or reverse burn-out. When you're working in your Zone of Genius, even if you have a hard deadline, you are less likely to feel stressed because you will be tackling your work efficiently using your strengths, as well as employing methods of work that you enjoy. It's when you are spending your time doing something that isn't fun and requires an enormous amount of energy that you'll get burned out. When you enjoy what you're doing because you're naturally good at it (i.e., in your Zone of Genius), you feel energized, not exhausted, from your work.

I know it doesn't always feel like it, but everyone has a choice about the way they want to spend their days and exert their energy. The real sadness comes when people are living lives that they feel like they have not chosen. You can choose to be less stressed. You can create your own version of success. The energy that it takes to be proactive and take control of your life is the same energy it takes to grind through a life you don't love. Wouldn't you rather use your energy in a way that makes you happier? To do that, you need to take control of, and then maintain and enhance, your energy levels.

THE DETRIMENTS OF STRESS

The stress response begins when the hormone cortisol is released. Cortisol curbs functions that are considered to be nonessential or detrimental in a stressful situation and affects the regions of your brain that control mood, motivation, and fear. The long-term activation of the stress-response system—and the subsequent overexposure to cortisol—can put you at increased risk of numerous health problems, including anxiety, depression, digestive problems, headaches, heart disease, sleep problems, weight gain, and memory and concentration impairment.

When you consider the health implications of living a stress-filled life, it almost seems like a no-brainer to ditch doing what you hate in favor of the work that will reduce stress and bring you joy. Yet, having a job that looks good on paper, wins you accolades with your peers, and provides a great lifestyle, but stresses you out and isn't enjoyable, is still an accepted norm.

Why Poor Sleep Is the New Smoking

In the business world, sleep is strongly associated with weakness, and even shame. I've seen many businesses where the employees brag about who gets less sleep. Sleep scientist Matthew Walker says, "We have stigmatized sleep with the label of laziness. We want to seem busy, and one way we express that is by proclaiming how little sleep we're getting."[36]

Achievement junkies succeed in the work world by staying late at the office and forgoing sleep. They might complain about the long hours, but it's a badge of honor to say, "I've been in the office until eleven every night." That's how some people judge how effective they are, even if those hours are not well spent. There are also many company cultures that buy into this idea that longer office hours equal loyal employees.[37] However, a 2015 study from John Pencavel at Stanford University found that employee output falls after a fifty-hour workweek and is dramatically reduced after fifty-five hours. Worse, those who work a whole extra day a week are literally wasting their time: the research shows that those who put in seventy hours a week produce nothing more than those who work fifty-five hours.

Whenever I speak in front of small and large groups, there are often only a few people in the room who will admit to getting enough sleep when I ask. There are countless stories of workaholics who have found their way to the very top of their fields, but what we don't often hear about is the fact that they've sacrificed everything in order to get there, including relationships, family, joy, and sleep. And what about people who have gotten to the very top of their fields and *do* get enough sleep? They exist. Why don't we ever hear about them? Because it's not part of our culture to walk into the office and say, "Oh yeah, I totally got eight hours of sleep last night!" That is something we need to change.

Arianna Huffington shares her story of burnout in her first book, *Thrive*. One day in 2007, Huffington, who had been working eighteen-hour days building the Huffington Post website (now known as HuffPost), was at home on the phone and checking emails when she passed out, fell down, and woke up in a pool of blood, with a broken cheekbone and a cut over her eye. After weeks of medical tests, doctors finally came back with a diagnosis: she was exhausted.

Working yourself to the bone is one model for success, but it's not the most successful model. In her second book, *The Sleep Revolution*, Huffington discusses how damaging poor sleep can be. Because of the myriad health problems associated with it, poor sleep has become a public health emergency. Our cognitive functions are impaired without proper sleep. One aspect of this is that our emotional intelligence is degraded, so we are more likely to overreact and become irritable. There's even research connecting sleep deprivation to mental health problems and depression.[38] Huffington calls the perceived benefit of working late into the night a modern delusion and writes, "Yet the myth persists that we can do our jobs just as well on four or five or six hours of sleep as we can on seven or eight." According to Rina Raphael, a writer for *Fast Company*, a loss of sleep not only impairs employees' moods and diet, but also hinders productivity, creativity, and decision-making.[39] For most jobs, exhaustion generally leads to subpar performance, whereas in fields such as medicine or transportation, sleep deprivation can mean life or death to innocent bystanders. Clearly, getting good sleep should be a priority for those who want success. If you're looking for ways to give yourself more energy during the day, start there.

In his book *Why We Sleep*, Matthew Walker suggests that dreaming is a soothing balm.[40] Scientists have long known that during sleep, memories are consolidated. However, Walker shows that we also sleep to forget. During sleep, we deactivate the emotional charge of our daily experience, making it easier to address the following day. Without good sleep, getting back to the office can become unbearable.

Walker takes his sleep incredibly seriously, and so should you. He states, "I give myself a nonnegotiable eight-hour sleep opportunity every night, and I keep very regular hours: if there is one thing I tell people, it's to go to bed and to wake up at the same time every day, no matter what." Improving your sleep hygiene can be this simple. The harder part is realizing that you have a problem. You can feel better about prioritizing sleep over other work activities that aren't substantially helping your career.

How You Spend Your Time Is Everything

More than fifty years ago, the pioneering sleep researcher Nathan Kleitman discovered the *basic rest-activity cycle*. These are the ninety-minute periods at night during which we move progressively through five stages of sleep. Kleitman also observed that our bodies operate within the same ninety-minute rhythms during the day. When we're awake, we shift from higher to lower alertness.[41] Some refer to this cycle as our *ultradian rhythm*.[42] The body responds to this cycle by sending us a signal that we need to take a mental or physical break: we just need to be aware of it. Fidgetiness, hunger, drowsiness, and loss of focus are some of the signals. When we work without taking a break for more than ninety minutes, we begin to draw on our emergency reserves by stressing out—releasing the stress hormone cortisol—which provides a little bit of an adrenaline rush to keep us going. The problem is that many of us have become addicted to the stress reaction. Or, we've unconsciously trained ourselves to override these signals, using artificial ways to pump up our energy: caffeine, foods high in sugar and simple carbohydrates, even exercise.

When we take these cycles into consideration, it becomes clear that, contrary to popular belief, we can't have optimal thinking by sitting at a desk from nine to five. The Energy Project was started by business writer Tony Schwartz. He writes about the value of monitoring your energy and taking breaks. He speaks often about how the nine-to-five model doesn't sync well with our brains.[43] He believes, as I do, that it's not productive to work in long stretches, and it's not possible to engage in our best thinking by pushing through and working all day long. In order to optimize the output and quality of your work, you need to take breaks.

If you're an individual contributor or a new employee, or your company has strict opening and closing times, you may not be able to set your own hours. To optimize your thinking and productivity, make sure you're getting enough sleep when you're not at work and that you're prioritizing your well-being. You can do this by taking time off from work and incorporating calming daily activities that are nourishing to the mind and body. Yet lots of people tend to do the opposite. They get off work, socialize, and stay up late because that's their only free time, and then their energy at work the next day is minimal. And what I've noticed is that these individuals aren't getting joy or building confidence at work, which is another reason their free time seems so valuable. It's the only time they feel free. Most of us are operating on cruise control and aren't able to recognize how our lifestyle is impacting our performance at work. But once you start operating within your Zone of Genius, you'll find the joy you're looking for during the day so that you can relax at night and get the restful sleep you need. When you create work you love, you'll find that it's easier to focus on prioritizing your energy and your well-being so that you operate as best as you can during those work hours.

I had a client named Stan who recognized that whenever he would go out partying, the next day at work he was off his game. He was tired. He didn't think as clearly. He was a little bit hungover. He felt like he was caught in a cycle of bad habits. I had Stan start using the Performance Tracker, which really helped him shift his behaviors. At the end of every week Stan would enter into the Tracker the nights he would go out drinking and how he rated his performance the next day. He was able to see a pattern: whenever he had more than two drinks he felt foggier at work and more unbalanced the next day. He also felt more anxious and tired. He also noticed that he drank more coffee on those mornings, which probably accounted for his jitters and increased anxiety. As a result of seeing that data he realized, *I just have to stop drinking during the workweek. I want to be clearheaded, and the nights I drink are affecting my ability to do my best thinking the next day. Even on the weekends I want to slow down, so I'm only going to have a drink or two at most.*

Many people feel that they are at the mercy of the workday, but

I would argue that we can be proactive about our schedules. People get locked into following the rules without considering the fact that they have options. However, most managers would agree that we can and should optimize our workday to match our productivity schedule. While it's easy to get into a habit of doing the same thing day in and day out and doing what everyone else around you is doing, if you know that a different solution is better for you, speak up! You may just be surprised how flexible work can be.

Another suggestion I make to my clients is not going to all the meetings they are invited to. A lot of people feel that if they're invited to a meeting they have to go, rather than looking at the agenda and thinking, *Do I have to be there? Is my contribution essential? If someone else from my team is there, I don't need to go.* This one small change can create up to six, eight, or even twelve additional hours a week for some people. If you're in a more junior position, again, talk to your manager. Map out how much time you're in meetings and what value you're getting from them. If you can make a case that some of the meetings aren't a valuable use of your time and that you could accomplish more by not being there, you could get the go-ahead to skip them. Even if you don't get permission to opt out of the meetings, the exercise in and of itself is a useful way to demonstrate your ability to be more self-directing with your time and energy.

All of these suggested strategies point to a switch to thinking *I am in charge of myself* versus *I am at the mercy of someone else.* People struggle with prioritizing their well-being because they've bought into the idea that they are more productive and a more valuable employee if they are at work longer and sacrifice their well-being. Reversing this thinking requires developing the practice of taking ownership of your time. Let's talk about some strategic ways you can begin to do this now.

Create Your Ideal Workday

I always ask my clients what their ideal workday should look like. Many answer with really specific requests:

- "I'd really like to have a couple of hours in the morning to be thinking about my day. Then, I want to have a couple of hours of meetings. Ideally, there's clear deliverables of that meeting, and then I want to have a few meetings with my team."

- "Ideally, I would like have all of my meetings, at most four, in the mornings. In the afternoon I would have two hours of uninterrupted, alone time to think, and then a separate time to check emails."

- "My ideal day begins with a workout, then two hours of thinking time and checking emails at home. I would then go into the office feeling refreshed and ready to tackle meetings with my team and with my colleagues. Then I end the day with a final hour of alone time to think about my priorities for the next day."

Then I ask, "How different is your current day from your ideal workday?" Most often, everyone's real day is completely different from what they would like it to be. The most common complaint is not having enough time to think, spending too much of the working day in meetings, and feeling like they are constantly in reactive mode due to the constant bombardment of new work.

My task is then to help them create that ideal workday as often as possible so they are getting more time to think instead of reacting or structuring their day to be more energizing. Sometimes, it means implementing very simple changes, such as leaving the office to work in a café or staying home for an extra hour in the morning to do some thinking. Or in some cases when a company allows it, to work from home once a week. If that's not possible, it can be as simple as going to the company cafeteria during non-meal times and using it as a place to sit and work uninterrupted. Or it could mean initiating walking meetings for a boost of energy. Arianna Huffington talks about how walking meetings made a huge difference for her workday enjoyment and are also a great way to get some fresh air while doing business.[44] Most of my clients report back that these small changes make a huge difference in their overall energy levels and well-being when they are in the office.

My client Tonya is the CFO of a small start-up business who never felt like she could leave her office. It took her three years until she realized that the business kept growing and moving forward regardless of whether she was in the office all day. Now she spends Friday afternoons at a café catching up on her industry reading. She tells me that one small change has shifted her energy and ability to have some focused time to herself, and it has become her favorite part of the week.

My client Mary, who is in an entry-level position, struggled to focus at work because people were always coming over to her cubicle to ask questions or just chat. She found that by reserving a small conference room for one afternoon every week on a different floor from her department gave her some uninterrupted time to get through her low-priority tasks. She also created a simple sign for her desk that let people know when she was free to talk and when she was doing focused work. Both of these strategies helped Mary feel like she had more control over her workday.

Try this exercise on your own. Think about what you really want your day to look like, and then think about what it would take to get there. This is the first step to prioritizing your well-being. I bet you'll see that with just a few small changes you can craft an ideal workday—or at least get a few steps closer.

Exercise Will Boost Your Genius

One way to boost your brainpower is through exercise. According to researchers at the Mayo Clinic, exercise pumps up your endorphins, which are your feel-good brain chemicals and can give you the mental resilience to thwart overreacting to stressful situations.[45] Exercise also improves your mood. Mayo researchers found that regular exercise can increase self-confidence and decrease symptoms associated with mild depression and anxiety. Lastly, exercise can improve your sleep, which is often disrupted by stress, depression, and anxiety.

I would not be where I am today without my workouts. Since I was a kid, I have religiously worked out five days a week, and that has continued into my adult life. It's a commitment that has become part of me. My workouts give me daily energy and confidence, and are a vehicle for my competitive spirit. I also do some of my best creative thinking when I'm active. I will go into a workout with a problem that I am processing, and by the end the answer has come to me. I see working out as a key partner to my ability to be in my Zone of Genius.

Find workouts that are fun so that you will look forward to them. There is an endless variety of workouts, and many will match your personality, and even your genius. For example, because my genius is an Insight Excavator, I create ways to gather data from my workouts. I have a Fitbit and love looking for patterns from the data. It makes working out more fun for me.

If you're an introvert, you may find that working out solo is more fun than doing classes at the gym. If you struggle to commit to a workout schedule or are an extrovert who enjoys exercising with others, hire a trainer or find a workout buddy who will help with accountability. I have hired trainers many times, and because I'm an extrovert, it makes working out feel like a party.

Of course, you should always consult with a doctor before starting any new exercise program, and if you haven't exercised in a long time or just had a baby, start slowly. Regardless of your ability to continue or start a workout routine, keep in mind that exercise is one of the best ways to increase your energy and give your brain the boost you've been craving. If you haven't exercised in a while, it's easy to forget the power that it wields. You can approach it like everything I've suggested in this book: make sure it's aligned with you and your body and is fun and challenging.

Meditation Is a Gift

Bill George, Harvard Business School professor and the former CEO of Medtronic, wrote, "The main business case for meditation is that if you're fully present on the job, you will be more effective as a leader, and you will make better decisions."[46] I agree, and the Genius Habit is all about being present. The more present you are at work, the more likely you're able to notice the changes you need to make in order to grow.

Meditation can be an excellent skill to learn for those battling anxiety and high stress. I suggest it to most of my clients, and many who incorporate it into their lives experience a positive shift. Even if you can't meditate every day, it's a practice that is free and easy to do, so there's very little downside to giving it a try.

Meditation is also an effective technique for building the Genius Habit because it helps fine-tune your ability to slow down and take notice of your thoughts. I like to think of it as taking your brain to the gym. The act of focusing on a single mantra (a common meditation practice that involves repeating one word over and over) trains your brain to focus your thoughts. This doesn't mean that meditation is easy: it is called a "practice" for a reason. However, in time you will realize how much unnecessary angst is happening in your brain. This ability is crucial when it comes to the focus required to staying in the zone. As Arianna Huffington wrote in *Thrive*, "Meditation can help not only focus, but also refocus after being distracted—which is an increasingly common peril of our technology-besieged lives."

I learned how to meditate from my friend and meditation coach Andre Elkind, who practices the Ayurvedic approach, which includes having a mantra. Andre suggests trying two fifteen-minute sessions each day for optimal results. For those who can't dedicate that much time, one session a day is better than nothing at all. If you want a tool to support your goal of meditation, check out Headspace, a great app that can help you start small and work your way up.

Setting Boundaries Helps Preserve Your Energy

Now that you know what may be draining your energy through bad habits and have reviewed some methods to get it revved up again, it's important that you protect the time you're devoting to these new practices. Setting boundaries is a great way for you to honor your new habits and ensure that they become a part of your life, rather than something that is quickly forgotten. By making the time to get better sleep, exercise, and meditate, you are already setting boundaries by prioritizing your needs.

Additionally, if you believe a particular boundary is part of what makes you who you are, you can take a stand for it. When you're clear with other people about why you're setting this boundary, it's unlikely that it will hinder you from achieving what you want.

For example, many people assume that having a consulting business means meeting with people in person. However, after meeting with clients in person for over a year, I made the decision that meeting with my clients in person would not be the best thing for them or for me. It completely altered the way I operated: I had to dress a certain way, I had to have an office, and it eliminated my ability to work with people who did not live close by.

I also discovered that working remotely with clients is a better way for me to fully execute my genius. When I am on the phone, I am cutting out visuals, which can be distracting to my focused thinking. My genius requires me to listen intensely to what my clients say and then look for patterns. What I found that is when I am face to face with someone, my focus is not as acute. Ultimately, it's a disservice to my clients for me not to work in the environment that allows me to produce my best, most thoughtful work.

While some people may believe that you can't build a relationship without face time, I actually don't think that meeting my clients in person is ideal. When I am working with someone, I am there completely in service to them. In many ways, I want to be invisible. When I'm meeting with someone in person, reciprocity comes into play, and they feel like they have to ask about my life or give to me. The phone removes reciprocity and allows my clients to relax more into the relationship where I am the one giving and they are receiving. They also feel more comfortable telling me anything. Not to mention, busy clients rarely have the time to fit an in-person meeting on their calendars. Meeting virtually allows our sessions to fit into their schedules more seamlessly.

Ultimately, meeting with people over the phone not only suits my desired lifestyle but also gets me better results. When clients say, "I really wanted to work with someone in person," I share my thinking, and more often than not, they end up deciding to go with me. This is the power of knowing what conditions give you the most energy and the best results.

Boundaries serve as a tool to help you not only be more productive but also focus on what matters. Steve Jobs is a great example of setting boundaries with his wardrobe. He decided at some point in his career that all he was ever going to wear was black turtlenecks and jeans. For him, not having to think about his wardrobe saved that mental energy for decisions that mattered more to him. He took a stand for what worked well for him.[47]

Your Zone of Genius can absolutely inform the boundaries that you may want to create. Knowing your Zone of Genius allows you to communicate with confidence and clarity around what kind of work you're best suited for and be very clear about what kind of work is not aligned with who you are. When you can communicate clearly the work you are best at, you will be given more of the work you actually want to do. This conversation is not a natural one, but it needs to be done. Your manager is generally the one responsible for prioritizing the workload. Managers don't have the time to get to know the inner genius of everyone on their team—that's why it's up to you to let them know about your boundaries.

The Next Step

With your confidence created and bolstered by greater energy, it's time to tackle the final behavior: perseverance that's bolstered by grit and curiosity.

Switch Your Orientation Toward Work

Identify how well you're prioritizing your well-being. When you're not, find the times in your day when you can make a shift and improve your self-care.

1. How often do you find yourself making the trade-off between your well-being and working long hours at the office? How does this make you feel?

    _____

    _____

    _____

    _____

2. Do you believe that working more than fifty-five hours a week produces work that is of high value? Does being sleep-deprived or close to burnout put you in a state that you believe allows you to do your best work?

    _____

    _____

    _____

    _____

3. How do you feel when you are able to focus on your well-being? Do you see that your output is higher quality?

    _____

    _____

_____

_____

4. How often do you get enough sleep (eight hours of uninterrupted time in a bed)? If not often, why, and what can you do to change this?

_____

_____

_____

_____

_____

5. Is exercise a part of your life? If not, what type of workout is fun to you? Are you able to start that workout at least three times a week?

_____

_____

_____

_____

_____

6. If you're not prioritizing your well-being, why not? What is one well-being commitment that you can make now?

_____

_____

_____

_____

_____

PART V

PERSEVERANCE

CHAPTER 10

GET CURIOUS, BUILD GRIT, AND SEE ADVERSITY AS OPPORTUNITY

Question: How can you eliminate your fear of failure?

Genius Action Plan: Add Curiosity and Grit to Your Genius

I am not the first person to say that the only thing you can count on in life is change, but nowhere is this aphorism more true than at work. One day you love your job, the next day the company is sold and in comes a new manager who sees your position as nonessential. Or you're recognized for doing a great job by being handed a promotion, only to find that the new gig is a bad fit for your genius. Change can also come from within: after years of doing the same thing every day and feeling relatively fulfilled, you suddenly find your job uninteresting and want a change.

There are hundreds of scenarios that could put you in a position where you're facing adversity in your career. While new challenges at work will inevitably present themselves, it's up to you to find a way to see these challenges as opportunities. The reward for doing so can be a game changer.

I believe there are two core behaviors we need that will allow us to persevere in difficult times: grit and curiosity. Grit ensures that you never give up no matter what happens, and curiosity allows you to be open to change and new ideas. What links them together is that they both require the kind of effort that leads to innovative thinking, which is the best way to create new opportunities and deal with adversity.

Adversity Is a Necessary Part of Success

Most people have a laundry list of failures. In fact, if you've never failed at anything, I would question your ability to persevere and step outside your comfort zone. It's not important how often you fail or even necessarily why you failed—what's important is how you deal with these failures. We've all heard that what doesn't kill you makes you stronger: adversity is the creation of opportunities. But sometimes it's hard to see the silver lining when you are deep inside the clouds. Big disappointments or setbacks should give you pause, but it's important to remember that they are also learning opportunities.

When adversity hits, you have a choice: you can quit or feel defeated, or you can get curious about what you can learn from the experience and choose to move forward and innovate to figure out another solution. This process of first being curious and then persevering to come up with a new solution is an essential behavior pattern that is required for success.

When you are curious, you become a type of explorer. You are in a constant state of discovery, which helps keep the gears in your mind turning so that you can be both creative and innovative. Dr. Todd Kashdan, a professor of psychology and senior scientist at the Center for the Advancement of Well-Being at George Mason University and the coauthor of *The Upside of Your Dark Side*, writes that when you are truly curious, your mind expects to be surprised. You don't assume any one particular answer or response, and you are prepared to fully take in diverse opinions.

Getting curious opens your mind to possibility, which is the breeding ground for ways to pivot from adversity. Once you've come up with a new approach, you can cultivate another powerful perseverance tool, grit. Angela Duckworth's groundbreaking book, *Grit*, was one of the first to show that focus, perseverance, and passion are key components to success that have often been overlooked. She states, "Enthusiasm is common. Endurance is rare." Having grit means no matter what comes your way, you will continue to operate at full speed; your effort is not diminished by the circumstances. Grit is developed during those times when you want to give up but don't.

Because the Genius Habit allows you to accomplish more with less effort, I believe that operating within your Zone of Genius is a necessary precursor of grit. It's easier to face adversity when you deeply engage with work that is aligned with who you are, as opposed to being constantly worn down by everyday tasks that feel onerous and burdensome. I like to think of any major challenge you might face as the last mile of a marathon. How prepared will you be to face that last mile after having run the first twenty-five miles through quicksand, fighting for every step? It would be easier to run that final mile after being set up for success—running on a flat, paved surface, with plenty of water and snacks available. Working within your Zone of Genius is the equivalent to running in perfect conditions—there is effort involved, but it is minimal compared to what it could be under unfavorable conditions—and it allows you to face adversity with more resilience and ultimately persevere longer than you would be able to if you were already exhausted.

I have experienced firsthand the way the Genius Habit can promote grit. After the first couple years of building my business, I wanted to make a big shift from working with small business owners to focusing on getting new clients from the corporate world. It was a natural evolution given that I had spent eleven years in the corporate world myself and had an extensive corporate network. However, shifting my business to focus on this new demographic was daunting; it was almost like starting over.

One of the first corporations I booked was Capital One, and the deal came together so quickly that I assumed I would be able to book a few more companies easily within a couple of months. Boy, was I wrong. I got curious and learned quickly that booking a company as a client could take anywhere from three months to three years. My business pipeline started to dry up, and while Capital One was proving to be a great resource for me, I was only able to identify a handful of clients every six months.

This was a make-or-break situation for my business. I could have become overwhelmed with the enormity of the challenge. Or, I could double down, focus on being curious, and then figure out an action plan, which is exactly what I did. First, I created a sales process that was running at all times. Previously I had only focused on sales until I booked a client, and then I would have to stop and focus on working with them. In the new plan, I hired a sales support person and designed a systematic sales process. This allowed me to keep seeking new opportunities even when I had a full client load. I also readjusted my expectations. I knew that it would take time and a lot more work to book more companies. I dove in and cut back on my expenses until I could sign a deal with a big client. My goal was to get at least one person in a large company to work with me. Once the company saw the results that individual was able to achieve, it would likely promote my services to other employees.

My curiosity and grit paid off. I slowly started connecting to the corporate leaders who hired outside resources. I never gave up, even though for every door that opened there were twenty that closed. I kept reaching out to individuals at the companies I wanted to work for by suggesting a LinkedIn connection. Once that connection was secured, I built a relationship. Knowing that it could be a year before I got actual business from the people I connected with, I started writing articles for *Inc., Forbes,* and *Fast Company* to help me build my brand as a performance expert. These articles opened up more opportunity. I set my sights on specific, well-known business executives to feature in my articles. The interviews allowed me to connect with these corporate leaders, which sometimes led to me building strong relationships that seamlessly turned into clients over time.

By creating a sales process that could function on its own, I was able to focus on the work that was fun for me and linked to my genius—interviewing potential clients—which led to developing a client roster of companies. Looking back, it's clear to me that the challenge of building a more robust sales process for finding clients was a big win but took a lot of work, and that I would not have been nearly as prepared to face it if I had been exhausted and burned out. A result of having the Genius Habit ingrained into my daily process gave me the energy and perseverance to move beyond this adverse situation and into a new realm of success.

Curiosity Leads to Innovation
by Embracing Diversity

In this day and age, innovative new solutions come from embracing diversity. The workforce simply looks much different than it did even ten years ago, as people are more comfortable authentically presenting themselves. This is a huge step forward for civil rights, and the benefits don't end there. Research shows that not only does a diverse workforce benefit individual employees, but it also makes a company function better overall. Simply put, diverse teams cultivate better ideas.

In a study published in the journal *Innovation: Management, Policy & Practice*, researchers found that companies with higher percentages of female employees were more likely to introduce radical new innovations.[48] In another study published in *Economic Geography*, the authors concluded that increased cultural diversity is a boon to innovation. They pooled data from 7,615 firms that participated in the London Annual Business Survey. The results revealed that businesses run by culturally diverse leadership teams were more likely to develop new products than those with homogenous leadership.[49]

Yet sadly, many organizations struggle to execute their diversity and inclusion goals, because it's hard to do. The human brain is hardwired to fear differences, a phenomenon known as an *implicit bias*. In other words, despite our best intentions, we prefer to stick with others who look or think like us. Similar unconscious biases exist over different genders, the elderly, and various minority groups. These biases come from the brain's need to see patterns in things that are complex, and to categorize the world in order to simplify it. Whenever we encounter another person, the brain rapidly tries to figure out if he or she is friend or foe, and one cue our brains use to determine that information is whether the other person looks, acts, and behaves like us. This can be both a conscious and unconscious behavior. Just look at your Facebook and Twitter feeds. Are you following a divergent group of thinkers, or are you following a crowd that is morally, politically, or even artistically aligned with your current thinking?

Most people initially respond to differences with fear, judgment, and criticism. Yet this behavioral pattern doesn't serve us or the companies we work for. Innovation requires us to be able to work effectively with people who may be different, in the way they look, the way they live, or the way they think. So instead of being closed to change or differences, I suggest we get curious about exploring why someone would think differently or be different than we are.

Jerry Trampled Adversity

Jerry was one of those people who appeared to have it all. He was Ivy League–educated and had a résumé packed with great positions at some of the biggest consumer products brands. To top it off, he was a great guy.

We started working together when he left the corporate world and took a job as the head of human resources at a mid-size tech company. The problem was twofold. First, the job itself ended up being significantly different from what had been presented during his interview. Second, the company was a bad cultural fit for Jerry. The CEO had an overbearing personality, which was quite different from what Jerry was used to. Jerry's genius was a Collaborative Vision Strategist. He was exceptional at creating visions that synthesized other people's ideas by collaborating with each person and then creating a new strategy that matched the needs of each person but served the whole. It was a genius that was well suited to a strategic HR position, but because this company was still growing, it just wanted him to recruit and hire new employees. The work that needed to get done was more logistical in nature than what Jerry had been led to believe.

Jerry clearly wasn't happy in this job, yet he wanted to prove to himself that he could succeed in the start-up world. Like so many people, he found the idea of quitting hard to wrap his head around, especially since he had just started. But every day it became more obvious that the job was a bad fit, and his disconnect with the culture was causing him anxiety and frustration. Not too surprisingly, the company made the decision for him.

For Jerry, being fired was more than a disappointment. He

had great hopes for this job, and while he knew deep down he wasn't right for the job, getting let go was a huge hit to his ego. I helped him see that what seemed like a disaster was actually an opportunity. Now he could find a job that was the right fit and one in which he would be valued for his strengths and be able to work within his Zone of Genius.

We began a strategic job search, focusing on roles that were aligned with his genius and would provide him with enough growth so that he could stretch his vision-making capabilities. We also made a list of cultural red flags that had been present in his last company. This time around he would be able to recognize whether the organization would be the right fit. We also created specific language for him to use in interviews that allowed him to articulate clearly what he brought to the table and provide examples of how he would do this, with plenty of options depending on the company and its challenges. I instructed him to use the following phrases:

"I am fulfilled by helping people feel acknowledged, so much so that I have been featured in articles about how I acknowledge others through my leadership. I would like to bring this expertise to your company."

"I see that you are in need of an HR leader who can bring together the executive team. My core strength is doing just that. In fact, meeting with individuals, hearing them out, and then creating goals and plans that are a reflection of everyone's needs is my expertise. I think this could be helpful for some of the challenges you've been experiencing."

Jerry realized that getting fired did not make him feel as though he needed to change who he was. Instead, it emboldened him to be more of who he was for the next opportunity. He wanted to deepen his HR experience, not widen his focus. Within three months he found a job working for another technology company in a role he was much better suited for. The company was larger and at a point where it needed to develop its people, and it needed a strategic HR leader to figure out how. It was one of the fastest job hunts I've ever helped someone through. He stayed in the same industry, and he gained clarity on what kind of HR leader he was, and because he understood his genius, he was able to articulate the value that he could provide in his new role.

For Jerry, the unforeseen adversity of being in the wrong company and getting fired turned out to be a big opportunity. He displayed grit by not giving up, learning from the situation, and committing to finding another opportunity that was better. This is the magic of grit—the more practice you have at not giving up on yourself, the less likely you will do it at all. He also demonstrated curiosity by opening his mind to possibility and looking at the interview process as a way to learn about other organizations and to interview them just as carefully as they were interviewing him.

He learned that a job hunt is also a time spent learning as much as you can about future opportunities. From now on Jerry will be able to see future rejections as opportunities and stepping stones to something better.

Get Out of Your Comfort Zone

Everyone says, "You need to get outside your comfort zone." But what does that really mean? Are they suggesting you should work against your genius? I hope not: if math is hard for you and it's never been something that comes naturally, becoming an accountant is probably going to be exhausting and stressful.

To me, getting out of, or stretching, your comfort zone means identifying ways for you to exercise your genius at the next level up from where you're currently working. It also applies to your approach to adversity. It means not giving up, and being gritty, innovative, and curious in how you move forward—all with your Zone of Genius in mind.

The Performance Tracker will help you see when you've hit a plateau; it's then up to you to proactively find the opportunities where you can stretch your capabilities to the next level. I tell my clients it's a good practice to proactively stretch your comfort zone so that when adversity strikes, you're practiced at being pushed in uncomfortable ways. The key is looking for the opportunities that are an extension of your genius or purpose and fearlessly tackling them. I am always proactively looking for more challenging client situations or working with groups in order to take my Insight Excavator genius to the next level. When my Performance Tracker tells me that I am not stretching my comfort zone, I set aside time to make a list of ways to do so and then direct my energy toward those new opportunities. Building perseverance and grit involves actively creating the scenarios that exercise your "never give up" muscle and making sure your new goals are aligned with your Zone of Genius.

Public speaking has always been a fear of mine. I would get so nervous about speaking that I wouldn't sleep for days beforehand; just thinking about it would make me sweat, and my hands would get clammy. Despite this fear, being a professional speaker has always been a dream of mine because I knew it would be a great way to have an impact that's meaningful to me. If I can help a whole group of people see themselves for who they are at the same time, I know I'm doing the work I'm meant to do. What's more, I have always loved attending events to hear speakers, as well as listening to TED talks. I had even been to some of the early TEDx events in New York City and knew that the process of getting chosen to speak at one was difficult and competitive.

A friend of mine knew my work and was on a planning committee for a TEDx event. He suggested that I apply to be a speaker. The good news was that I got the gig. The bad news was I only had a month to prepare. My whole body started sweating, and I got sick to my stomach. Having a TEDx talk would set me up for getting other great speaking opportunities. I needed to nail it.

I hired a writing strategist to help me create a talk that I would be proud of. Then I practiced my speech every day for two weeks straight, probably three times a day. I practiced until I couldn't practice anymore. During a TEDx talk, you aren't allowed to use notes, there's no teleprompter, and there is a camera on you at all times. And the videos that go online are not edited; everything has to be perfect in one take. My nerves were so intense that I didn't eat for three days prior to the talk. Instead, I did breathing exercises and meditated.

By the time I was supposed to present, I felt like I knew what to do. My legs were shaking as I walked onstage, but as soon as I started talking, all of the practice kicked in. The adrenaline high of actually doing something that scared me so much made me feel energized. By the end of the talk, I felt amazing, and I knew I had nailed it.

I am very proud I took on the challenge of that TEDx talk. Every step of the way felt like I was pushing myself to the limit, and now I know that the more I push my comfort zone, the more I discover what I'm capable of. Since then, I have had the opportunity to speak in front of small to large groups in a variety of environments. Back then I was not what I would call a professional, but stretching myself has given me more confidence in my speaking abilities, and every time seems to be easier than the time before.

Stepping Out of Your Comfort Zone

Creating opportunities to get curious and step out of your comfort zone is not easy. You must actively find the opportunities that scare you and then face that fear head-on. Answer the following questions to get yourself in gear for taking your skills to the next level:

1. What are some activities that you've secretly always wanted to do but are terrified of? Make a list.

    _____

    _____

    _____

    _____

2. Which of these activities are linked to your genius or purpose?

    _____

    _____

    _____

3. What can you start doing now to take significant action on one of the activities you listed above? How can you be accountable?

    _____

    _____

    _____

After you've accomplished the first activity, think about tackling the others. When you're feeling bored or complacent, refer to this list to get ideas for stretching your comfort zone.

Deepen Your Focus and Become an Expert

One of the more positive aspects of persevering is the opportunity to deepen your focus within your Zone of Genius. This can lead to the acquisition of or honing unique skills that are highly valuable to employers and enjoyable for you to practice. The ability to focus is what gets you in the zone in the first place, but when crisis hits, many people don't know where they should place their focus. I can't tell you how many ambitious people find themselves stuck because they don't know how to focus or what to focus on. In an attempt to push through the adversity, they choose to spread their energy in a variety of directions, throwing ideas against a wall hoping one will stick. This lack of focus can be overwhelming and ineffective.

In cases like this, let your genius help. By relying on your genius, you can dive into the problem with the singular problem-solving skill that you're already good at. By returning to this skill every time you run into a challenge, you will naturally develop an expertise. Then, when the unforeseen happens, you don't have to question your value, who you are, or what you should be doing. You can simply focus on solving the problem with your well-honed genius.

According to Anders Ericsson, researcher and author of *Peak: Secrets from the New Science of Expertise*, it takes an average of ten thousand hours of focused, deliberate practice for anyone to become an expert.[50] The question I often ask my clients is, "How much fun are you going to have if you're spending more than ten thousand hours toward something that isn't aligned with your Zone of Genius?"

I believe that deliberate practice—which involves creating a structured system of practicing and tracking your results—is a meant to be a joyful journey. One example Ericsson shares is how tennis players use deliberate practice. The secret to getting better isn't playing more tennis matches against a variety of opponents. It's the repetitive training drills and exercises that make your game stronger. It's pushing yourself and stepping out of your comfort zone every time you hit a plateau. But if you don't enjoy the drills to begin with, and if the challenge of the game itself isn't aligned with your genius, you are never going to put in the hours to take your game to the next level. However, if you are building grit around something that initially is joyful, you can become one of the best at it with a focused deepening of expertise and time.

The reward of focus is becoming an expert at something you love. This is how I know that I have found my calling. Using my genius as an Insight Excavator in my work as a performance strategist while helping individuals be seen is the work that feels like an extension of who I am and who I want to be.

Genius Action Plan: Add Curiosity and Grit to Your Genius

Cultivating grit by facing adversity with perseverance and curiosity while staying true to who you are may be something new to think about:

1. What was your last big disappointment? Did you address it by being true to yourself and using your Zone of Genius? Did you deal with it with curiosity? Did you get gritty in how you moved through it? If so, what did you learn from it and how can you be more curious or build your grit for the next time you are faced with adversity?

2. When was the last time you stretched your comfort zone and felt powerful after? Were you using your genius? What's preventing you from taking those same actions or using the same type of thinking to stretch it again?

3. Can you list some work-related projects you could tackle that would take you out of your comfort zone? What would it take for you to start tackling each one?

4. How gritty do you think you are and how much more so do you want to be?

Hunter Used a Crisis to Get Curious and Build Grit

My client Hunter came to me in the midst of a life crisis. He had just been fired and felt that he had been discriminated against because he struggled with alcoholism. He was told that he was fired for his poor performance, but the reasons given were trivial and he did not believe them to be valid. Hunter had been at his company as head of retail sales for twenty years, and although he struggles with addiction, he had been a great employee who was recognized over the years with multiple promotions. He hired a lawyer who believed Hunter had a strong case of workplace discrimination. The lawyer also suggested that Hunter start looking for a new job. Hunter had a choice: he could wallow in self-pity and mourn the job he had lost, or he could move forward, build grit, and persevere. He chose the latter and hired me.

My primary goal with Hunter was to help him begin to see this adversity as an opportunity. We talked about how he could focus on finding a new job in which he could stretch himself out of his comfort zone and refine his focus. I suggested that he become a spokesperson and advocate for alcoholics and help organizations understand how to better support these employees rather than ostracize them. Hunter became very excited about the prospect of using his job loss as an opportunity. The thought of becoming a spokesperson energized him, and his belief in himself grew. It was clear to me that he was determined not to give up.

Hunter's genius was helping others think outside the box and improve their outcomes; his purpose was making the impossible possible. He approached the research phase of his job search with curiosity and discovered that jobs in diversity and inclusion are a fast-growing subsection of the HR industry. There would be tons of opportunities to help companies figure out how to best serve minority groups or underserved groups that feel like they have to hide who they are at work for fear of retribution. We crafted a plan of action, and he began applying to this type of role in large and midsize companies where it existed and pitching it to those organizations that didn't have this type of role but clearly needed it. We also clearly mapped out how a diversity and inclusion position at an organization was a perfect fit for his Zone of Genius and how he might leverage his unique outlook to become an invaluable resource in this newly created position.

The act of taking his career into his own hands helped Hunter move past his crisis and regain his confidence. He learned that even though his life was not going the way he would have ideally wanted, he was more resilient than he had ever realized.

The Next Step

The next chapter will help you use your Zone of Genius to find the next best job. Changing jobs can help you continually evolve and, over time, enhance your focus. It becomes a lot less scary to leave a job, or look for a new one, when it's clear who you are and what value you bring to the table.

CHAPTER 11

EMBRACE THE JOB SEARCH AND THE UNKNOWN

Question: Should I quit my job?

Genius Action Plan: Become a Job Search Ninja

If you are unhappy at work, remember to look for the root cause of your discontent. Earlier in the book you learned that if you are failing at your job, you're likely in the wrong job. If you have determined that your job matches your Zone of Genius, even if you are facing adversity in your work, you feel confident that there is still an opportunity for you to be challenged and fulfilled by the job you're already doing. That is a great sign that you can dig in and persevere. There are, of course, other variables at play other than the work itself. You could be in the right job but have a bad cultural fit, terrible colleagues, or a company that won't give you the autonomy you desire. Or, there may come a point where you simply say, "Is this still the journey I'm supposed to be on?"

The key to knowing when to quit is to clearly identify what is causing your desire to leave. Once you know what that is, you can assess if it's a situation that requires grit to work through and resolve, or one that can't be resolved at all.

Here is a list of rational reasons for you to leave your job, rather than fight the good fight:

1. **Culture isn't the right fit:** Company culture is a challenging thing to change. You won't be able to tackle this with grit unless you're the head of HR or a chief people officer. And if you are, you'll still need to have buy-in from the entire executive team. Unless that is the case, changing a culture is not a realistic endeavor.

2. **Challenging manager or colleagues:** The people you work with dictate your environment. If you feel that the majority of the people you work with aren't people you enjoy or are people you just can't get along with, it's probably a sign to move on. With that said, it's important to know your unconscious biases and work to resolve conflicts with others if they arise. Conflict is often an opportunity to learn more about yourself and someone who is different from you. If you're the only one making the effort and your manager or colleagues refuse to be open-minded and work

with you to resolve conflicts, then you will know it's time to move on.

3. **You are being harassed, manipulated, or don't have psychological safety:** Psychological safety is being able to be yourself without fear of negative consequences.[51] If you can't be yourself, or are being harassed or manipulated, it's a no-brainer—it's time to take action. In the world of #metoo, women are taking back their power with their voices and their feet. If you experience mistreatment in any form, you should communicate it to HR and move on if it is not handled appropriately and swiftly.

4. **The company moves in a direction that is in opposition with your career vision:** When your career prospects start to veer away from the vision you have, take action.

Keep Your Career Vision in Sight

Envision your career as a road map: it helps you plan your route to get you where you want to go and corrects your course when you get off track. I believe that having a vision is a requirement for career success. The key to ensuring that your vision continues to evolve is to revisit it often, especially after a significant achievement. With the amount of change that happens in business these days, an inflexible long-term vision only leads to disappointment. However, when you're focused and in your Zone of Genius, you will find that you will most likely achieve your vision faster, which will offer you the opportunity to continually think bigger.

Your vision is likely to change slightly with each new job, even if you change positions within your company. If you are faced with an unexpected job search, you can view it as an opportunity to review your overall vision. The more you match your Zone of Genius to your vision, the more resilient you'll be and the easier it will be to find a new job that you'll love.

What's Your Career Vision?

Take a step back—look for your vision in your answers. You can create a short-term vision and then a long-term plan. I think having both is not only fun but also can help you stay grounded in your desires and on your path. Remember, you will review and alter your vision frequently, so don't get hung up on it being perfect. It must be inspiring and exciting and feel true to you.

Take out a piece of paper and write down your answers to the following questions.

VISION QUESTIONS

- What's working for you in your career now? What's not?
- What's your vision for your family life and the amount of time you spend with them versus work?
- What do you want your legacy to be in your current organization or industry?
- When do you want to retire?
- What does retirement mean to you? What would a day of retirement look like?
- Do you want to make more money? What is the lifestyle that you desire? (Think about this question carefully since we know external things don't provide fulfillment or happiness.)
- What does freedom mean to you?
- Do you want more authority?
- What level of impact is important to you? Are you looking to make a big or small footprint with your work?

- What kind of people do you want to be working with and for?
- If you are contemplating a job change, what are the absolute must-haves?

Take a few minutes to read through and reflect on your answers above. Now, fill in the following:

My short-term vision (three to five years) is:

_____

_____

_____

_____

_____

_____

_____

_____

My ultimate long-term vision (the objective of your entire career) is:

_____

_____

_____

_____

_____

_____

_____

_____

Apply the Genius Habit to Your Job Search

Being able to navigate a job search seamlessly is imperative in the changing landscape of work. While a job search can be intimidating, you need to get used to the idea because you will have to go through the job interview process many times over the course of your career. Gone are the days when most people stay with the same company, or even the same industry, for their entire careers. To find the right new job, you need to become a job search ninja. A job search ninja is fearless about the prospect of navigating a change, and you are confident in your value—so if it's clear that things aren't ideal in your current role, you start the job search with excitement and a plan. The less fear you have about changing jobs, the more powerful you will be in terms of guiding your career toward your vision, and in the direction that you want to go.

I've met many people who avoid the job search entirely and stay in jobs they don't like because they are overwhelmed at the prospect of searching for a new one. They simply don't know where to begin and don't understand the process, especially regarding the ever-evolving way that technology and social media have changed the way companies recruit new employees. They are unprepared to face the rejections that invariably come or the arduousness of deciding what to look for. They also lack clarity on how to speak about themselves, what value they bring, and what they are looking for.

Once you know your Zone of Genius, there will be infinite

possibilities for you to explore, yet sometimes it's the infinite pos-sibilities that make finding a job so daunting. The job search is an area in which you can use your genius and your purpose to narrow down your search. Start with organizations or types of work that are meaningful to you. Is there an opportunity for you to directly impact another person who is aligned with your purpose? Is the company delivering or creating a product or helping people in a way that's connected to your purpose? If not, keep looking.

Once you have identified areas of work or companies that may be a good fit for your purpose, look at the specific jobs and the potential roles that could use your genius. Use the kind of thinking and problem-solving that you're best at and compare your genius to job opportunities. When you land the interview, you can find out more information about how often you would be able to use your genius on a day-to-day basis. If the job has no opportunity for you to use your genius, it's not the right job for you.

Lastly, try to get a sense of the culture at any company you interview for. A sense of connection with the person you would be reporting to is a great place to start in terms of figuring out whether you would be a good fit for the team. Many people take jobs they think will look good on their resume. Or they have waited so long to start looking for a new opportunity that they are burned out on their current job and take the first job offer that comes their way. But if they are so desperate to leave their old job that they don't take the time to properly vet the new company and manager, they'll likely end up right back where they started—unhappy and looking for a way out.

Have faith that the right opportunity will come your way, and until then, dig into the process and do a lot of work. I have clients who come to me in despair saying they left their previous position and can't find a job; then I find out they're only reaching out to two or three companies a week, when they should be targeting ten, fifteen, or twenty. If you're not working, a job search should be your full-time job. If you're still employed, expect to do less job hunting work each day and recognize that the process of finding the right job will take more time.

If your job search is taking longer than you expect, get curious. There are probably areas of the interview process in which you can improve, such as how you're presenting yourself or how thoroughly you're interviewing a potential employer. Use your search to build grit, and never give up. There are endless opportunities. If you embrace the process as an adventure rather than a chore and become skilled at speaking about yourself, you will end up finding opportunities that you never thought were possible.

Reference Your Zone of Genius at Every Interview

Understanding your Zone of Genius and knowing how to explain it effectively can dictate how you speak about yourself and your value to others. When you get to an interview, I wouldn't necessarily encourage you to say, "I'm going to tell you what my Zone of Genius is," since many people won't understand the terminology, but you can talk about your thinking process, what you bring to the table, and how you've identified the type of work that is meaningful and motivating to you. Being able to articulate those three ideas can be impressive to an employer. Employers are looking for highly motivated, hungry individuals. If you can explain what it is that makes you an asset, all the better. And if you can connect that self-knowledge to the role you're applying for and show how your thinking motivates you, it would be hard for someone to be dismissive of that level of preparation and self-awareness.

Consider broaching this subject in an interview by saying something like, "One of my biggest strengths is that I know myself. I know how to be proactive and get work done. I know the work that I'm best at. I know the kind of thinking and problem-solving I'm better than anyone else at, and it just so happens that this is what seems to be required for this role. And I know that in this role I will be endlessly motivated because the impact that this company is having is personally motivating to me. I'm also comfortable with managing my own career and managing my performance, and I will regularly tell you how well I'm performing, what's working, what's not. If I'm managing a team, I will help my team members develop the habits of managing their own performance as well."

This ability to be both firm and clear is hard, and at first you may find it a little awkward to speak so confidently about your abilities. However, speaking up for yourself is part of the Genius Habit, and if there's anything on your resume that requires more explanation, such as a history of changing jobs or a gap in your employment, it's helpful to be able to speak clearly and confidently about your past opportunities and experiences, what you bring to the table now, and how you see yourself offering and bringing value to the job that's available.

Each time you speak about yourself, observe the reaction of the interviewers. Do they seem to understand and appreciate what you're saying? This is how you can tell that they also see how your genius is of value to the new role and the organization.

Building Your Brand

Creating and managing your brand by including what you're an expert at—your Zone of Genius—is another way to make a job search less cumbersome. If someone Googles your name, what comes up? Make sure the search results reflect what you want to be known for.

Your brand is something you need to be building throughout your career, not just when you are out of work or deep in the job search process. If you haven't done the work to create your brand yet, start thinking about ways you want to be known. If you're struggling to land on a brand strategy, one course of action could be to hire a brand strategist if you have the resources to do so. Having someone walk you through the process of helping you communicate what you represent to the world is a great gift to yourself. Provide the strategist with your Zone of Genius, and they can help create a communication strategy that should be fun to execute.

If you're more the DIY type, there are a number of ways to start the process. Your LinkedIn profile is a building block for sharing your brand online. Blogging sites such as Medium, Tumblr, and Squarespace give you endless opportunities for creating content that is aligned with your expertise. The act of creating this content in the form of blogs or articles and posting it on your feed, along with commenting on others' posts, helps you create a brand identity and a virtual footprint, which is what comes up when people Google you. Your virtual footprint is how others develop a first impression of you and what you do.

Your brand also comes through in the way you speak about yourself and your work in professional situations. When you meet new people, how do you quickly describe what you do? Being consistent with what you say and how you speak about yourself is another way to bolster your brand.

Genius Networking

If you're an introvert, just the idea of networking may send shivers down your spine. However, while building your professional network is an essential aspect to finding a new job, it doesn't have to be tortuous. In fact, I have helped the biggest introverts figure out ways to network with joy. Today more than ever your network is a solid key to getting the right job. Why? Because while technology can provide access to lots of opportunities, it also means that more people are applying for every job, and companies are inundated with stacks of resumes with no real knowledge of who these people are. People who do not know the best strategies for finding a job revert to submitting their resume online to company after company. Unfortunately, that's often met with very little response. If you're applying for a job along with a thousand other applicants, winning an interview is just as likely as holding a winning lottery ticket.

Today, a resume is nothing more than a business card, and blindly submitting it is not an effective way to approach a job search. Instead, making the effort to build relationships so that you are more than just a resume in a pile is essential. Rather than submitting your resume and letting it talk for you, you can do the talking for yourself through networking.

Think of networking as opening the door of opportunity to your career future. This includes meeting people who not only can offer you a new position, but also can expand your thinking. People usually don't network until they're out of work, and when you have to do it in a pinch, it's a less effective strategy than networking all the time and making it part of the way you operate in the business world.

When I work with clients, we start just like you have, by identifying their Zone of Genius. Then we build out a vision so that we understand where they want to go, what's not working where they are, and what the absolute must-haves for their next opportunity are. At that point, I suggest making a list of companies or organizations that they're interested in working with. Then we take the list of companies and match them with their existing network, such as their LinkedIn connections, alumni association, or previous colleagues. You start by going over the people you know to see if anyone you're connected to is somehow connected to one of those organizations.

Then step out of your comfort zone and reach out to people you don't know at all. Connect with people who work at the company you're interested in. Reach out to the hiring manager. Reach out to the business leader you'd be working with. Tell them why you're interested in the job. Set up a fifteen-minute phone chat: very few people can't make time for that. If you're clear on your career vision and you're clear about what you're an expert in, you can start to interview people or talk to people about their perspective on that work. Remember to be respectful of their time and clear about your objectives. "This is why I'm reaching out to you. This is what I would love to talk to you about. Are you interested?" If there is someone in your organization you want to learn from, make the meeting social by saying, "Hey, I'm interested in the work you're doing, and I'd love to learn more about it. Let's grab a coffee or have a twenty-minute phone conversation during our lunch break."

Be thoughtful and strategic about how you reach out to people. I'm amazed at how many LinkedIn requests I receive that do not include a personal message. Sending a LinkedIn request without a personal note is pretty much like walking up to someone on the street, poking them on the shoulder, and saying, "Hi, will you be my friend?" It's ineffective and feels invasive. The more thought you put into your networking, the more successful you will be with it, and the more likely it is that others will see a mutually beneficial reason to connect.

The goal is to continuously build connections and relationships with people you can help, and in turn they will be willing to help you. Think about what you can offer these people: *What can I bring to the table that might make them interested in meeting with me?* Use your Zone of Genius as a starting point to tell them about your brand. By using your genius and your purpose as a lens, it is easier to talk with a headhunter or job search professional to explain exactly what you are looking for.

A lot of people believe that networking means attending job-focused events or career fairs and meeting with people face to face, but I believe that's a limited strategy. It's very time consuming going to events, and for some it's not that fun.

Others worry about putting someone on the spot or that they are a bother. But I've found that if you have a compelling and clear reason why you want to connect with someone, that person will be responsive. This is especially true for recent college graduates; if they show initiative, most people are willing to meet with them and will be generous with their time. All you have to say is, "I'm a recent college graduate and I'm really clear on what I am best at and what value I can offer. This is the work I want to be doing. I'd love to learn from you and figure out where I should be applying."

If you are at a later place in your career, networking is all about initiative while being creative. What's something interesting that you've done? What conversation can you bring to the table that the person you want to connect with may be interested in talking about?

GETTING GREAT JOB SEARCH INFORMATION

There are a ton of books and online information to help you in your job search. Here are some of my favorites:

Websites for job searches and search management:

- JibberJobber
- LinkedIn Job Search
- Indeed
- CareerBuilder

Websites for job search information:

- Job-Hunt
- The Muse
- DailyWorth

Books for job searches, career advice, and mind-set:

- *Pivot: The Only Move That Matters Is Your Next One* by Jenny Blake
- *Steal the Show* by Michael Port
- *The 2-Hour Job Search* by Steve Dalton
- *The New Rules of Work* by Alexandra Cavoulacos
- *Tribe of Mentors* by Timothy Ferriss
- *The Quarter-Life Breakthrough* by Adam Smiley Poswolsky

Are You a Job Search Ninja?

Use these prompts to determine whether you are ready to tackle the challenge of a job search:

1. When do you think you will have to conduct another job search?

   _____

2. What scares you the most about your next job search? What scares you least?

   _____
   _____
   _____
   _____
   _____
   _____

3. After reading this chapter, what areas of the job search do you need to focus on the most in order to feel more fearless?

   _____
   _____
   _____
   _____
   _____
   _____

CHAPTER 12

YOUR GENIUS WON'T CHANGE, BUT YOU WILL

Question: How will my genius evolve over time?

Genius Action Plan: Use the Performance Tracker
to Track the Evolution of Your Genius

Your Zone of Genius is never stagnant, and neither is your career. The more your work allows you to be in the zone, the more your genius will evolve and your expertise deepen. For instance, my genius as an Insight Excavator allows me to synthesize information. By using this focused approach for doing the work I'm best suited for, I literally can see and feel my expertise deepening. I've also found that this ability works faster and more efficiently every time I use it, and I require less information to come up with an answer.

You may already see some subtle shifts in the way you are

working, but many people can't really see their expertise sharpening because it happens so gradually. This is where the Performance Tracker really comes into play. Your evolution will become more apparent to you with this single habit, because tracking is the most systematic way to show how and when you are using your genius and building your performance behaviors. The Tracker provides the vehicle for you to not only reflect, but also plan ahead—it's the routine part of the habit loop. The reward is your new awareness that comes from following this routine week over week. Taking action from that awareness is the Genius Habit that allows anyone to achieve greatness.

Depending on your seniority and your job, you can share the information you gather with your team, manager, or colleagues. The Tracker is in essence a performance evaluation that you're giving yourself every week. You're already doing the work that you would need to do in order to provide your manager or your team an update on how things are going for you. It allows you to clearly see reality, not what you may think or by making false or erroneous conclusions based on feelings that ebb and flow. So not only is it a habit for your own success, but it's also a habit that will transform you into a superstar employee.

Create a Plan for Communicating Your Genius

Many of us expect our managers to pick up on what we're good at and assign us projects that use our strengths. While managers can make an educated guess and share opinions, your current job will be more fulfilling and challenging when you are vocal about how you can best use your Zone of Genius. It is powerful for you to say, "This is what my genius is, and this is how you can leverage me to achieve your goals." Remember, it's in your company's best interest to maximize your performance, so you're helping them—and yourself—by cluing them into your Zone of Genius.

Another important practice to start incorporating is setting up Zone of Genius performance discussions with your managers and colleagues. This is a great technique for building relationships within your company. Working with others who are operating in their Zone of Genius will boost morale while making it easier for each of you to focus on the areas in which you thrive.

When embarking on a job search, be explicit about how you see yourself in the open position and give a detailed explanation on how you would tackle the challenges that job presents. In interviews, we tend to generalize when talking about ourselves because we're afraid of coming across as a bad fit for the job, but it's far more influential to be specific with the interviewer about what you're good at and what brings you fulfillment. Employers value workers who know their own strengths and how to use them.

It's also valuable to communicate your weaknesses. We often are advised not to do this, but I have found that it is of great benefit for a potential employer to know what you're not good at. The most effective strategy is to present your weaknesses in terms of how you overcome them. For example, I am a terrible speller, and I will never pretend to be great at it, but I make sure to use a variety of tools to double-check my spelling before I send emails or documents to clients. Writing is an important aspect of my work, and I have found a solution to ensure that I deliver accurate products 100 percent of the time. Let go of the idea that you need to be great at everything—just have a plan to tackle your weaknesses that doesn't involve you trying to be who you're not.

What to Expect When Filling Out the Performance Tracker

You won't have to fill out the tracker for the rest of your life. After a while, you'll start to inherently observe the elements that are causing and preventing great performance and be able to make changes on the fly, not three months down the road. If after three months you've mastered the tracker and you want to take a break, great. Then bring it in again when you start to feel like your performance is off. It's there for you when you need it. I still use the Tracker pretty frequently, but I don't use it every week because the habit is so ingrained in me. Yet when I feel a little bit off, I dive back into it week over week so that I can get clear as to where that feeling is coming from and make the necessary shifts to reorient me.

You will find that by filling out the tracker, over time your awareness of who you are deepens, and you'll have a better understanding of how things are operating in your current job regarding your performance and how you're operating in your current role and organization. You'll be able to identify the root causes of any frustration or discontent. You'll also become aware of what's creating the joyful moments, the excitement, and the great things that are happening in your job.

What's more, you'll notice that your awareness improves, and you'll be better equipped to tackle your negative mental chatter and areas where you lack confidence. You'll become more aware of your triggers, and with the other exercises in this book, you can continue to deal with and ultimately reverse the power these triggers hold.

SEE HOW FAR YOU'VE COME

After a month of focusing on your Zone of Genius and completing the Performance Tracker, go back and review your performance and see how much you've changed. If you are using the electronic version from my website (lauragarnett.com), there will be an Excel tab for each week. The snapshot feature creates a graph of all your scores. What you then have is a record of how you've scored on each principle over time. This can be really insightful because you can see which areas you may still need to focus on. You'll also see when you're not in your Zone of Genius and when you are really on fire.

Consistent negative scores in the Tracker can signal problems, trends, and patterns. Rather than making major decisions—like quitting your job—in the heat of the moment, you have a longer-term, less biased view to make decisions from, which ultimately gives you more control over your career.

FEEDBACK FROM PERFORMANCE TRACKER FANS

Here's a glimpse into the discoveries a few of my clients made while using the Performance Tracker:

Filling out the tracker on a weekly basis has been an effective mechanism to stay disciplined on tracking my goals, how I could have handled specific situations better, and what actionable steps I can take the following week to improve my performance. During the daily grind of work, it can be difficult in the moment to stay mindful, but increasing self-awareness and performance takes practice, and the weekly trackers have been a great exercise while events are still fresh in my mind.

—Quincy Yang, Head of Business Operations at OpenTable

One of the key things that can differentiate a good leader from a great one is being self-aware of who you are, what your strengths are, and where you have downfalls. Having a personal tracker can feel cumbersome and formal, but taking time to write down what's going on in the busyness of each week can be a valuable way to become more self-aware. I found that by earmarking time regularly to reflect on my performance, it empowered me to make the needed changes to maximize my impact. And after a while, the habit led me to be more conscious day-to-day, and I was naturally more mindful of my performance without needing an official tracker to remind me.

—Heather E., VP of marketing

Use the Tracker to Plan for the Future

In chapter 10, you created a vision statement for your career, and you can use the Performance Tracker each time you revisit this vision. You can continually use this habit to create the career changes you want and drive the success and greatness you desire. By tracking your joy and the days you're operating in your Zone of Genius, you can gauge whether you're having the experience you want and if your current job is taking you closer to your ultimate vision.

Remember, your vision can be malleable, but having one will provide clarity and provide direction, especially when you navigate job changes. The more you stretch your comfort zone and the more proactive you are with your career, the more likely your vision is going to expand over time. I've seen this with some of my top clients: their visions change every year because they achieved the vision they set and now they have to go bigger. You'll also be able to see whether your vision still excites you.

Use the Tracker for Your Next Performance Review

The traditional performance review is usually an annual or biannual process that involves getting detailed feedback from your peers on your performance and having your managers provide you with a score that determines your ability to be promoted or given a raise. These performance reviews take a lot of time and energy to complete. When I was at Capital One, for example, there was a full week or two that was spent in meetings around the performance review, looking at people's scores, and coming up with a bell curve for raises and promotions.

The traditional process evaluates a small snapshot of your performance because most people can't remember more than a few weeks or a month out. Then this snapshot is applied to the past six months or even the entire year. If, as a manager, you're waiting six months or a year to really dig into performance, you're not effectively developing people. This is one of the reasons why, more often than not, performance issues don't get resolved, or they are resolved with quick fixes that don't work because the actual problem has not been diagnosed correctly.

Many companies are completely doing away with the traditional performance review and moving toward a more agile, more frequent, check-in process. Instead of receiving a score, you may engage in a less formal conversation. The reason for this is that performance is something that should be assessed on a regular basis, and obviously how someone performs in January might be vastly different from how they perform in October.

This new trend requires individuals to be more responsible for tracking their successes and failures. The good news about this new system is that it mirrors what life is like outside of an organization and in many ways is more entrepreneurial. If you're a consultant or running your own business, you have to be able to motivate yourself and continually stretch your comfort zone in order for your business to grow. In the past, large organizations have traditionally let managers determine the future of their employees. This new way of operating forces everyone to adapt and learn how to manage themselves. The bad news is that a lot of people don't know how to be introspective. They're used to the system of their performance being dictated by a manager.

With the practice of job-hopping on the rise, individuals must become the CEO of their own careers. I believe that knowing yourself, managing your career, and tracking your performance are all critical to long-term career success in our current and future business environment. The Performance Tracker is an ideal tool that will help instill the habit of both knowing yourself and identifying the root causes of what's happening with your performance.

In addition, great companies to work for are increasingly seeing the value in investing in their people. Cultivating the careers of the internal team is much more cost-effective than always seeking new talent from external sources. I've found that employees who are familiar with their performance strengths and weaknesses and can self-correct while having a clear idea of where their career is going are the ones who are considered the superstars.

Can You Be the Ideal Employee?

I talk to hiring departments of some of the best companies to work for (companies that are walking their talk and creating people-first cultures), and I'm constantly asking them to define what their dream employee looks like. Across the board, they tell me that experience matters less, while the ability to collaborate well with others, think differently, and clearly lay out who they are and what value they offer matters more. The bottom line is that anyone can gain experience, but not everyone is able to know themselves, take initiative, work well with others, and be proactive. These are the functions and the ways of operating that are required to come up with the best ideas that employers are looking for.

These are also the exact behaviors that come from practicing the Genius Habit and using the Performance Tracker. This way of operating will help you be the best version of yourself, which is what translates into becoming an ideal employee. If you can clearly convey that you know yourself, your strengths, and your weaknesses; can be proactive with your performance; can work collaboratively with many types of people; and are open, curious, and innovative with your thinking, who wouldn't want to hire you?

Can You Be the Ideal Leader?

I have repeatedly seen that working in your Zone of Genius creates great leaders. First and foremost, great leaders need to know themselves. They also put their people first. They know that truly great results and progress come when their team members are happy, feel safe, and are heard and actively involved. They engage others around them and don't worry about being center stage all the time, all for the good of the company.

You can inspire others by sharing this process. If you are a manager or team leader, knowing what you're great at is important, and it will be of even more value if your teams are equally self-knowledgeable. This is one of the best ways to really get to know your coworkers. The more you know your team members, the better you'll be able to inspire them and leverage their abilities. This greater connection between you and your employees also will help build trust and psychological safety, which leads to a more open and positive working environment in which people are not afraid to speak up about their ideas and are encouraged to be innovative in their work.

Rich Sheridan, CEO of Menlo Innovations and author of *Joy, Inc: How We Build a Workplace People Love* and *Chief Joy Officer: How Great Leaders Elevate Human Energy and Eliminate Fear*, has received tons of accolades for being a forward-thinking leader. He speaks all over the world on how to be a great leader. In fact, he calls himself the Chief Storyteller. He sees the role of the CEO as bringing people together and facilitating collaboration and decision-making. He doesn't make unilateral decisions, and he doesn't think of himself as the one in charge. In fact, his version of leadership is all about ensuring that he's facilitating his team to operate at their best and lets them make their own decisions. This kind of leadership is indicative of what companies are moving toward. When you're not telling people what to do, it opens the door for each of them to own their Zone of Genius and advocate for the work that is right for them. This type of communication is key for people to operate at their potential, and a leader like Sheridan is all about making that a priority.

A great leader makes it a priority to help their team navigate the process of prioritization. When team members can each identify their Zone of Genius and use the Performance Tracker, they can take ownership of their performance. Then, the team can easily share how they will approach the work you want them to do and get better results because the work is matched with the right person to do the best job. They also can tell you when the assignment isn't aligned with their genius, which helps the quality of work remain high. If you allow the "bad fit" conversation to be commonplace, you're more likely to avoid poor outcomes and mediocre performance—a killer to a business's success.

Lastly, a great leader isn't spending their time micromanaging or being a career counselor for the team. I see a lot of managers who think they are doing their employees a favor by helping shape their careers. While ambitious, it's actually burdensome. Instead, you can encourage your team to manage their careers by using the Genius Habit in this book. Then, you can maintain and even enhance the environment that allows your people to be who they are and create the work that's right for them.

Peak Performance Can Be the Norm

Once you make it a habit, operating within your Zone of Genius becomes a way of life, not something you achieve once and then move on. It's a new way of thinking and observing how and why you do what you do. Now it's your responsibility to implement these habits and achieve a new level of consciousness every day. With this heightened awareness, you'll begin to notice when you're bored, when you're stressed, and when you're disengaged. Most importantly, you'll honor these feelings as valuable signs that you're not operating in your Zone of Genius and take the necessary steps to get back in the zone.

I hope you walk away from this book understanding the accessibility of achieving greatness through leveraging your innate strengths. The fact is, greatness is not for the few; it's for everyone. Each one of us can use the Genius Habit to bring forth our unique value and brilliance to the world. We each owe it to ourselves and to others to do the work that enables us to bring our best, most powerful self forward.

Whether or not you've experienced what it's like to have your dream job, trust that it is out there waiting to be discovered—or created. If doing work that you love is a priority and you remain diligent, there's no reason you won't end up in a position that is exactly right for you. When you get there, you'll find that joy at work is indeed possible, a reward you'll continue to enjoy for many years to come.

AFTERWORD

When I was at my lowest point, I'll never forget the thoughts that were swirling through my head. *What if I am not able to create something meaningful with my career? I feel like I have something special to bring to the world, but what is it? What am I meant to do? What is my next step, and how do I ensure that it's better than where I am now? I thought I had something big to do in my life; was I wrong?*

The powerlessness I felt was overwhelming. I had little support and I couldn't seem to find the answers I was seeking. There were hundreds of books that talked about what created success, but I couldn't find anything that spoke to the *how—how was I supposed to know what the first step should be?*

My hope is that by reading this book, you never have to feel the way I did. Once you begin the process of knowing your Zone of Genius and practicing the Genius Habit, those thoughts will disappear. And if those thoughts come back? That's the alarm to buckle down and dive into the Genius Habit process again.

In the end, this book is meant to teach you more about you. What has been so fascinating to me in my ten years of working with this material is that very few people are in touch with their greatest strengths. Seldom are they wielding the power that is readily available within themselves. That power increases when you build the Genius Habit.

If you do the work that is outlined in this book, I promise it will change how you feel about yourself and your career. When you fill out the Tracker every week, you will undoubtedly have one or more moments of saying, "Wow, I really see how my core emotional challenge comes up more than I expected" or "I'm really using my genius this week—this project is *exactly* the kind of work I need to be doing. Let me create more of this!" Or you could realize the job you're in is way better for you than you thought. Or maybe it's way worse than you realized. The more frequently you use the Tracker and internalize your new self-knowledge, the more the Genius Habit of unconsciously evaluating and correcting your performance will develop. Eventually, it becomes effortless.

I hope you also will experience more joy. Tapping into your purpose at work is like nothing you've experienced before. There is a relaxation that comes with this realization, which builds confidence about your career, and that confidence is magnetizing. You'll inspire others just by being who you are and doing the work you were meant to do.

My dream is that everyone will do the work to become an inspiration not only to themselves, but also to those around them. When joy, not drudgery, is associated with work, our society will be different. Living up to your true potential is the greatest gift you can give yourself but also the world. Enjoy the journey, and I hope it will become one of the most joyful experiences of your life.

APPENDIX

THE PERFORMANCE TRACKER

Think of the Performance Tracker as the Fitbit for your weekly performance. Keep monitoring and tracking it just as you might your fitness, sleep, or diet. Use the Tracker as a weekly check-in during which you track your ability to become more aware of your own performance and build the Genius Habit.

The time it will take to make the Genius Habit stick is dependent on your personality and how disciplined you are with using the Tracker. For the next two to three months, use the Performance Tracker once a week. If you prefer, download a version from my website, lauragarnett.com/thegeniushabit. This version comes with an algorithm that does the tracking and analysis week over week. However, the version in this book will get you the same results.

Find the day that works best for you. I always suggest Fridays, as you will be reflecting on the workweek that has just ended. Fill out the questions thoughtfully, reflecting on and reviewing your answers. You'll be rating your performance for each of the five core principles. You'll end up with a quantitative score as well as answer qualitative questions. The latter task allows you to reflect on your responses and come up with goals or agenda items for the following week. These goals allow you to improve your performance by implementing small changes or actions to help you operate more clearly in your Zone of Genius.

Take time to reflect on your experience and your impact at work. Answer each question thoughtfully and truthfully in the response section. Some questions will prompt you to enter a score—depending on the question, you'll be rating your effectiveness, frequency of an event, amount of impact, and so on, with zero being the lowest/worst score and 5 being the highest/best score. You'll use these numerical scores to plot your progress and compare across sections.

A score of 4 or 5 is ideal; anything less than that will help you pinpoint your challenges. Overall, a low score in section 3 (Joy) is the biggest indicator that you are not operating in your Zone of Genius.

Create a copy of the Tracker for each week and chart your total percentages in the graph at the bottom of the Tracker.

Scoring the Tracker

There are five sections in the Performance Tracker. To score each section, read each question and score yourself based on the scale provided. Place that number in the last column.

Score guidelines for determining your rating each week:

5 = Always

4 = 80 percent of the time

3 = 50 percent of the time

2 = 20 percent of the time

1 = 5 percent of the time

0 = Never

Add those numbers to get your total section score. Once you have that score, you can divide by the total number of points possible for that section to calculate your section percentage.

For example, if you are given two questions worth 5 points each and you scored yourself 4 points on each question, your total section score would be 8. Divide 8 by the total points possible; in this example, that is 10.

8/10 = 80 percent. Your section percentage would be 80 percent.

Note: Some sections require a negative score. For example, in section 4 (Mindfulness: Confidence, Growth Mind-Set, and Health), the second question asks you to rate your negative chatter from 0 to −5. In this section, even though there are four questions, the total possible score is 15. Divide your total score by 15 to calculate your final percentage.

Some questions only require a written response and no score. In those cases, the score column will be shaded.

EXAMPLE

Section 2 Questions:	Detailed Response	Score (0–5)
How would you assess your impact on others this week?	Input your detailed response	4
How much of this impact was in line with your purpose?		4
If the impact was not in line with your purpose, what can you do to shift this for next week?		
	Total Section Score:	8
		80%

Once you've calculated the total score for each section, add each of your five section scores to get a total score for the week. Divide the total score for the week by fifty to get your final percentage for the week. You can add your percentage numbers to the Peak Performance chart and the graph at the end.

1. CHALLENGE: ACCESSING YOUR GENIUS

Ensuring you're proactively using your genius

Questions	Detailed Response	Score (0–5)
Were you in the zone 0–5 times this week?		
What caused those moments to occur? Be specific.		
If none, what prevented you from being in the zone?		
What evidence indicates that you are making steady progress on the goals you've set?		
	Total Section Score:	
	Divide Total Score by 5	

2. IMPACT: MEASURING THE USE OF YOUR PURPOSE

Achieving the impact you desire

Questions	Detailed Response	Score (0–5)
How would you assess your impact on others this week?		
How much of this impact was in line with your purpose?		
If the impact was not in line with your purpose, what can you do to shift this for next week?		
	Total Section Score:	

3. JOY: AVOID BEING AN ACHIEVEMENT JUNKIE

Enjoying the process of executing your goals more than the achievement

Questions	Detailed Response	Score (0–5)
How much time this week did you spend on enjoyable work?		
How much time this week did you spend on boring or frustrating work? (Use a negative score here, 0 = no boring work at all, –5 = significant amount of boring work.)		
How effective were you at maintaining a 70/30 balance (70% exciting work, 30% not)?		
	Total Section Score:	
	Divide Total Score by 10	

4. MINDFULNESS: CONFIDENCE, GROWTH MIND-SET, AND HEALTH

Rewiring your thought process and being conscious of your mental chatter

Questions	Detailed Response	Score (0–5)
How confident did you feel this week and how often did you actively believe in your potential?		
How would you rate the amount of negative mental chatter you experienced? What prompted these negative moments? Record the trigger. (Use a negative score: 0 = no negative chatter, –5 = significant negative chatter.)		
How disciplined were you in actively rewiring your negative thought processes to support optimal performance?		
How effective were you at sleeping enough, exercising regularly, and prioritizing your well-being?		
	Total Section Score:	
	Divide Total Score by 15	

5. PERSEVERANCE: GRIT AND CURIOSITY

Cultivating grit and curiosity to navigate adversity and continually create opportunities

Questions	Detailed Response	Score (0–5)
How effective were you at never giving up and learning from your failures?		
How often did you face change or differences with curiosity rather than judgment?		
What distractions came up this week that prevented you from being focused and committed?		
How can you avoid that going forward?		
	Total Section Score:	
	Divide Total Score by 10	

| | TOTAL SCORE FOR THE WEEK | |
| | TOTAL % | |

PEAK PERFORMANCE: QUICK VIEW

For a snapshot view of the week, fill out the boxes below with your totals from each section

	Category	Effectiveness
	Challenge	
	Impact	
	Joy	
	Mindfulness	
	Perseverance	

Using the total percentages from your chart above, fill in the bar graph below so you can see your peak performance graphically.

Peak Performance

| 100% |
| 75% |
| 50% |
| 25% |
| 0% |

Challenge   Impact   Joy   Mindfulness   Perseverance

Now that you've filled out the Tracker, identify your lower scores. Write down five actionable ways to increase those scores in the upcoming week.

1. _____
   _____
   _____
   _____

2. _____
   _____
   _____
   _____

3. _____
   _____
   _____
   _____

4. _____
   _____
   _____

5. _____
   _____
   _____

ENDNOTES

1. Charles Duhigg, "How Habits Work," accessed April 26, 2018, http://charlesduhigg.com/how-habits-work/.

2. Phillippa Lally, Cornelia H. M. Van Jaarsveld, Henry W. W. Potts, and Jane Wardle, "How Are Habits Formed: Modelling Habit Formation in the Real World." *European Journal of Social Psychology* 40 (2010): 998–1009.

3. Sarah Cassidy, Bryan Roche, and Steven C. Hayes, "A Relational Frame Training Intervention to Raise Intelligence Quotients: A Pilot Study," *The Psychological Record* 61, no. 2 (2011): 173–198.

4. "Is a Happy Person More Successful at Work?" The Happy Manager, accessed April 26, 2018, http://the-happy-manager.com/articles/is-a-happy-person-more-successful-at-work/.

5. Drake Baer, "Why Incentives Don't Actually Motivate People to Do Better Work." *Business Insider*, April 1, 2014, http://www.businessinsider.com/why-incentives-dont-actually-make-people-do-better-work-2014-3.

6. "Putting a Face to a Name: The Art of Motivating Employees," Wharton School at University of Pennsylvania, February 17, 2010, http://knowledge.wharton.upenn.edu/article/putting-a-face-to-a -name-the-art-of-motivating-employees/.

7. Andrew Oswald, Eugenio Proto, and Daniel Sgroi, "Happiness and Productivity," *Journal of Labor Economics* 33 (2015): 789–822.

8. Staff writer, "Self-Confidence the Secret to Workplace Advancement," *The Melbourne Newsroom*, October 18, 2012, newsroom.melbourne.edu /news/self-confidence-secret-workplace-advancement.

9. McKinsey Global Institute, *Jobs Lost, Jobs Gained: Workforce Transitions in a Time of Automation*, December 2017, https://www.mckinsey.com/~ /media/McKinsey/Featured%20Insights/Future%20of%20Organizations /What%20the%20future%20of%20work%20will%20mean%20 for%20jobs%20skills%20and%20wages/MGI-Jobs-Lost-Jobs -Gained-Report-December-6-2017.ashx.

10. Chenkai Wu, Michelle C. Odden, Gwenith G. Fisher et al., "Association of Retirement Age with Mortality: A Population-Based Longitudinal Study among Older Adults in the USA," *Journal of Epidemiology and Community Health* 70, no. 9 (2016): 917–923.

11. Solomon E. Asch, "Effects of Group Pressure on the Modification and Distortion of Judgments," in *Groups, Leadership, and Men: Research in Human Relations*, ed. Harold Guetzkow (Pittsburgh, PA: Carnegie Press, 1951), 177–190.

12. Vasily Klucharev, Kaisa Hytönen, Mark Rijpkema, Ale Smidts, and

Guillén Fernández, "Reinforcement Learning Signal Predicts Social Conformity," *Neuron* 61, no. 1 (2009): 140–151.

13. "The Set-Point Theory of Happiness," ChangingMinds.org, accessed May 16, 2018, http://changingminds.org/explanations/emotions/happiness/setpoint_happiness.htm.

14. "Jung's Theory of Psychological Types," WatchWordTest.com, accessed May 16, 2018, http://www.watchwordtest.com/types.aspx.

15. Amy Adkins, "Majority of U.S. Employees Not Engaged Despite Gains in 2014," Gallup, January 28, 2015, https://news.gallup.com/poll/180404/gallup-daily-employee-engagement.aspx.

16. Adam M. Grant et al., "Impact and the Art of Motivation Maintenance: The Effects of Contact with Beneficiaries on Persistence Behavior," *Journal of Organizational Behavior and Human Decision Processes* 103, no. 1 (2007): 53–67.

17. Jackie K. Gollan et al., "Twice the Negativity Bias and Half the Positivity Offset: Evaluative Responses to Emotional Information in Depression," *Journal of Behavior Therapy and Experimental Psychiatry* 52 (September 2016): 166–170.

18. "What Is Tapping and How Can I Start Using It?" The Tapping Solution, accessed May 16, 2018, https://www.thetappingsolution.com/what-is-eft-tapping/.

19. "Our Commitment to Comprehensive Health Care," Starbucks Newsroom, accessed May 16, 2018, https://news.starbucks.com/views/health-care.

20. Grant et al., "Impact and the Art of Motivation Maintenance."

21. Grace Bluerock, "24 Quotes on Success from Oprah Winfrey," *Entrepreneur*, January 29, 2016, https://www.entrepreneur.com/article/269979.

22. Jon Terbush, "Roger Ebert's Most Memorable Quotes on Life, Death, and the Movies," *The Week*, April 4, 2013, http://theweek.com/articles /465866/roger-eberts-most-memorable-quotes-life-death-movies.

23. Alfie Kohn, "Why Incentive Plans Cannot Work," *Harvard Business Review*, September–October 1993, https://hbr.org/1993/09/why-incentive-plans -cannot-work.

24. Eric Barker, "How to Motivate People: 4 Steps Backed by Science," *Time* magazine, April 8, 2014, http://time.com/53748/how-to-motivate -people-4-steps-backed-by-science/.

25. Adam L. Alter et al., "Rising to the Threat: Reducing Stereotype Threat by Reframing the Threat as a Challenge," *Journal of Experimental Social Psychology* 46, no. 1 (January 2010): 166–171.

26. Jonathan Figliolino, "The Science of Stress Management: Your Brain on Cortisol," *I Done This* blog, March 20, 2017, http://blog.idonethis.com /science-stress-management-brain-cortisol/.

27. Joseph Lin, "Top 10 College Dropouts," *Time* magazine, May 10, 2010, http://content.time.com/time/specials/packages/article/0,28804, 1988080_1988093_1988082,00.html.

28. University of Leeds, "Go with Your Gut—Intuition Is More than Just a Hunch, Says New Research," *ScienceDaily* 6 (March 2008): https:// www.sciencedaily.com/releases/2008/03/080305144210.htm.

29. Justin Fox, "Instinct Can Beat Analytical Thinking," *Harvard Business Review*, June 20, 2014, https://hbr.org/2014/06/instinct-can-beat -analytical-thinking.

30. Jeff Bezos, "Amazon Founder and CEO Jeff Bezos Delivers Graduation

Speech at Princeton University," YouTube, posted June 11, 2010, https://www.youtube.com/watch?v=vBmavNoChZc.

31. Katty Kay and Claire Shipman, "The Confidence Gap," *The Atlantic*, May 2014, https://www.theatlantic.com/magazine/archive/2014/05/the-confidence-gap/359815/.

32. Deborah A. Small, Michele Gelfand, Linda Babcock, and Hilary Gettman, "Who Goes to the Bargaining Table? The Influence of Gender and Framing on the Initiation of Negotiation," *Journal of Personality and Social Psychology* 93, no. 4 (2007): 600–613.

33. Larry Kim, "50 Innovation and Success Quotes from SpaceX Founder Elon Musk," Inc.com, March 8, 2016, https://www.inc.com/larry-kim/50-innovation-amp;-success-quotes-from-spacex-founder-elon-musk.html.

34. Melissa L. Kamins and Carol S. Dweck, "Person Versus Process Praise and Criticism: Implications for Contingent Self-Worth and Coping," *Developmental Psychology* 35, no. 3 (1999): 835–847.

35. Cameron Anderson, Sebastien Brion, Don A. Moore, and Jessica A. Kennedy, "A Status-Enhancement Account of Overconfidence," *Journal of Personality and Social Psychology* 103 (2012): 718–735.

36. Rachel Cooke, "'Sleep Should Be Prescribed': What Those Late Nights Out Could Be Costing You," *The Guardian*, September 24, 2017, https://www.theguardian.com/lifeandstyle/2017/sep/24/why-lack-of-sleep-health-worst-enemy-matthew-walker-why-we-sleep.

37. Bob Sullivan, "Memo to Work Martyrs: Long Hours Make You Less Productive," CNBC, January 26, 2015, https://www.cnbc.com/2015/01/26/working-more-than-50-hours-makes-you-less-productive.html.

38. Hyong J. Cho et al., "Sleep Disturbance and Depression Recurrence in Community-Dwelling Older Adults: A Prospective Study," *American Journal of Psychiatry* 165, no. 12 (December 2008): 1543–1550.

39. Arianna Huffington, "Here's Arianna Huffington's Recipe for a Great Night of Sleep," Fast Company, June 10, 2016, https://www.fastcompany.com/3060801/heres-arianna-huffingtons-recipe-for-a-great-night-of-sleep.

40. PTV News, "'No Sleep Is for the Weak': Sleep Deprivation Leads to a Shorter Life," PTV News, September 27, 2017, https://ptvnews.ph/no-sleep-weak-sleep-deprivation-leads-shorter-life/.

41. Tony Schwartz, "The 90-Minute Solution: How Building in Periods of Renewal Can Change Your Work and Your Life," HuffPost, May 18, 2010, https://www.huffingtonpost.com/tony-schwartz/work-life-balance-the-90_b_578671.html.

42. Schwartz, "The 90-Minute Solution."

43. The Energy Project, accessed May 16, 2018, https://theenergyproject.com/.

44. Rebecca Adams, "Want to Make Meetings More Productive? Start Walking," HuffPost, May 18, 2014, https://www.huffingtonpost.com/2014/05/18/walking-meetings-productive_n_5333120.html.

45. Mayo Clinic Staff, "Exercise and Stress: Get Moving to Manage Stress," Mayo Clinic, March 8, 2018, https://www.mayoclinic.org/healthy-lifestyle/stress-management/in-depth/exercise-and-stress/art-20044469?pg=1.

46. Arianna Huffington, "Mindfulness, Meditation, Wellness, and Their Connection to Corporate America's Bottom Line," HuffPost, March 18, 2013, https://www.huffingtonpost.com/arianna-huffington/corporate -wellness_b_2903222.html.

47. Jacquelyn Smith, "Steve Jobs Always Dressed Exactly the Same. Here's Who Else Does," *Forbes*, October 5, 2012, https://www.forbes.com/sites /jacquelynsmith/2012/10/05/steve-jobs-always-dressed-exactly-the-same -heres-who-else-does/#492f5a95f53d; John Haltiwanger, "The Science of Simplicity: Why Successful People Wear the Same Thing Every Day," EliteDaily,November14,2014,https://www.elitedaily.com/money/science -simplicity-successful-people-wear-thing-every-day/849141.

48. Christina Diaz-Garcia, Angela Gonzalez-Moreno, and Francisco Jose Saez-Martinez, "Gender Diversity within R&D Teams: Its Impact on Radicalness of Innovation," *Innovation* 15, no. 2 (2015): 149–160.

49. Max Nathan and Neil Lee, "Cultural Diversity, Innovation, and Entrepreneurship: Firm-Level Evidence from London," *Economic Geography* 89, no. 4 (2013): 367–394.

50. Shana Lebowitz, "A Top Psychologist Says There's Only One Way to Become the Best in Your Field—But Not Everyone Agrees," *Business Insider*, February 14, 2018, http://www.businessinsider.com /anders-ericsson-how-to-become-an-expert-at-anything-2016-6.

51. Laura Delizonna, "High-Performing Teams Need Psychological Safety," *Harvard Business Review*, August 24, 2017, https://hbr.org/2017/08/high -performing-teams-need-psychological-safety-heres-how-to-create-it.

ADDITIONAL RESOURCES

I would love to help you solidify your Genius Habit. Here are a few great options for you to stay in touch and keep your Genius Habit going.

Stay Connected

Sign up for my free biweekly The Zone newsletter at lauragarnett .com, where I offer free Genius Habit check-ins (for tips as you read the book), and advice for your career questions, along with sharing my personal journey and insights as I continue to navigate my own career.

You can also follow me on Instagram @llgarnett for inspiring quotes and ongoing Genius Habit–building suggestions.

Go Deeper

Work directly with me: My genius is at its best when working with individuals one-on-one. I have a variety of individual packages. Visit lauragarnett.com/services to review how I can help you take your work performance to new heights.

Work with a Genius Habit coach: I have sought out and trained some of the best coaches I can find on the Genius Habit approach. If you are interested in learning more, please go to lauragarnett.com/services.

Have me be a select executive coach for your organization: I thrive when working with companies that are committed to their people and are supportive of them maximizing their potential. Visit lauragarnett.com/contact to reach out. It would be great to explore the opportunity to work with your executive team and your leaders to help them learn the Genius Habit and become superstars at work.

Speaking and workshops: I would love to come speak to your company or at your event. The Genius Habit talk or workshop is ideal for team off-site trainings, annual sales meetings, or any event that is focused on success or work performance. Please go to lauragarnett.com/speaking for more information.

INDEX

Mission and values statements (company), 130–131, 135

Money. *See* Extrinsic rewards; Golden handcuffs

Motivation
achievement junkies and, 154–158
extrinsic vs. intrinsic, 126–128
linked to purpose and impact, 18–19, 93–97, 128, 131–132
as necessary skill in business world, 22, 151–152
theories on, 94–97

Musk, Elon, 219–220

Myers-Briggs Type Indicator (MBTI), 73–74, 75

Myth of blissful retirement, 30–33

N

Nadella, Satya, 131

Naming your genius, 67–72

Negative feedback, 195–198

Negative habits, 7–9

Negative thoughts and emotions, 12, 21, 209
behavioral modifications, 113–115
threat environments, 161–163
triggers affecting your confidence, 210–215, 218, 226–227
See also Core emotional challenges

Networking, 288–292

O

Online brand, 288

Outcome vs. process, 151–160, 175

Over-preparedness, 211–213, 232–233

P

Partnerships, 185–186

Passion vs. purpose, 89–93

Patagonia, 97

Peak performance, 307–308, 321

Perfection at everything, as bad strategy, 211–213, 232–233

Performance
challenge vs. threat environments, 161–163
gender, and confidence gap, 215–217
happiness, linked to, 160–161
praising intelligence and, 222–224
principles for operating within your Zone of Genius, 18–22
problems, related to poor job fit, 24–28
See also Energy; Feedback; Job fit; Performance Tracker

Performance reviews, 13–14, 25, 76, 302–304

ACKNOWLEDGMENTS

Writing a book is very similar to giving birth to a baby. Ironically, I did both at the same time. My daughter Zoe was born in the midst of the writing process, and I spent the first four months of her life writing during her naps. Both births are incredibly miraculous and don't happen alone.

To James, my incredible partner in life, without your support, encouragement, and dedication to being the best dad ever, this process would have been impossible. I love you, admire you, and am the luckiest woman to have you by my side.

To Zoe, you are truly a miracle in every way, and your bright light has brought nothing but joy to both your dad and me. Your delight in the world reminds me to savor each moment, and watching you become who you are is the best gift I have ever received. You have been sleeping on me, with me, and next to me during this whole writing process, and I can't wait for your own genius to emerge and for you to take the world by storm.

My Book Team

My agent, Myrsini: from the moment we met, it was always meant to be. You have been one of the most joyous parts of this journey, and I love working with you. The ability to see potential and cultivate it is certainly your genius.

Anna, my editor, working with you has been a top work experience. Your speed, thoroughness, and ability to really "get" the work has been a godsend. This project would not be what it is without you.

Thank you to Sourcebooks and everyone there for being an ideal publisher. From welcoming me with open arms and rolling out the red carpet when I visited to diving in and giving me endless support for the entire book process to going above and beyond with marketing projects to support the launch of the book, I could not have asked for a better partner in bringing this book to the world.

Liz, your genius shines through with your marketing excellence. Thanks for the support, ideas, and assistance in getting this book out in the world in a meaningful way.

Pam, my writing partner. Thank you for your structure and your ability to literally pull parts of this book out of me that I didn't know were there. Having your hand guiding me through the process was a critical piece of its success.

Diana and Miranda, thank you both for your continual support and help. I love working with you both and couldn't do what I do without you. I love seeing both of your geniuses in action.

Marisol, thank you for your support at the beginning of this project and for your help in the editing phase. Your early involvement will never be forgotten!

Deidre, without your loving care of Zoe throughout the writing and development process, I could not have had the focus or time to do the work. Thank you from the bottom of my heart for all that you do for her and for us!

My Support Circle

I am lucky to have a network of powerful women who are not only good friends but also authors who have generously handed me nuggets of wisdom throughout the process:

Jenny Blake—you are so much to me that there aren't words to describe it. I don't think this book would be here without our talks and walks. You inspire me with your own genius in action continually.

Dorie and Petra, thank you both for offering up ideas and support throughout this process and even more for inspiring me with your greatness.

Cybele, thank you so much for your editorial feedback and

support for this book and me. It came at such a critical time, and I am forever grateful for your wisdom and deep friendship. Our walks throughout the birthing of this book fed my soul and filled my heart.

Gabby, I am so grateful for your support of my work, this book, and most of all, your friendship. I know this is just the beginning of so much more.

Erin and Kate, I love our babies and book club. The fact that we all birthed babies and books at the same time was magical. Thank you for your support, input, and sisterhood in being an author and a mother at the same time.

To Mom and Dad, thank you for giving me life and so much more, but most importantly for my ambition, my discipline, and my high bar for excellence. This book wouldn't have happened without those characteristics that I get from both of you.

To Julie, my sister, thank you for being my number one support system throughout the writing of this book; our daily calls gave me sanity, refuge, and clarity.

To my niece and nephews: Ella, Beck, and Connor—you are the future generation of our family, and your enthusiasm for life inspires me. I can see your geniuses emerging and the tremendous value that you have to offer the world. I can't wait to witness your greatness in whatever form it takes.

ABOUT THE AUTHOR

Laura Garnett is a performance strategist, TEDx speaker, and the creator of the Genius Habit. She works with CEOs and executives to identify their unique genius and purpose and craft an actionable plan to leverage them in their day-to-day work. She has consulted with organizations including Capital One, Pandora, LinkedIn, and Instructure. Prior to launching her own company, New York City–based Garnett Consulting, LLC, she honed her marketing, strategy, and career-refining skills at companies such as Capital One, American Express, IAC, and Google. Visit her at lauragarnett.com.

OPT-IN MONSTER.COM
PRICING